TWICE BROKEN

My Journey to Wholeness

ISBN: 0692696555
ISBN 13: 9780692696552

Library of Congress Control Number: 2016909835
TwiceBroken.org, Cranberry Township PA

Praise for
Twice Broken, My Journey to Wholeness

" Viewing catastrophic change in a positive light is surprising and powerful. Kathleen Serenko's honest and open approach to her own struggle gives voice and solidarity to women struggling under similar conditions. For any writer, let alone a new one, one of the hardest tasks is to combine intelligence with emotion. Ms. Serenko's story is one of ultimate triumph, not least as a writer. *Twice Broken* will undoubtedly be a success."

Denis Boyles, Author and Editor

TWICE BROKEN

My Journey to Wholeness

Kathleen Serenko

Dedicated to Dad and Mom,

for loving each other through thick and thin
and for freeing your children of the fear
that either of you would ever walk away.

With special thanks to Denis Boyles, who shared
his expertise without expectation and helped me
believe that my writing was worth sharing.

Introduction

Twice Broken: My Journey to Wholeness was supposed to be a story about divorce and the grief that follows. At least, that's what I had in mind.

For six years, I wrote, rewrote, and wrote again. I began my story at the point of divorce, and I wrote forward through the events and the heartache that followed.

Several years into the project, I began to write backward. By that I mean that I started at the point of divorce, but this time I wrote about the years and the circumstances that preceded it.

It took me all those years of writing to find my way back to the true beginning of the story. By the time I was done, the story of my life from the ages of eighteen to forty-eight was condensed into little more than a handful of pages. I never felt the need to write more, though. It was enough that I had finally identified the behaviors, the choices, and the consequences that had led me along that thirty-year journey from brokenness to wholeness.

For me it was a journey of personal revelation, as I uncovered how much of my grief was rooted in the physical and emotional abuse that had occurred decades before. Identifying that connection to the past, however, did not negate the depth of grief that accompanied my divorce and the years of struggle that followed.

The brokenness engendered by divorce remains central to the theme of this book, and for that reason it is still the best way to introduce the story of *Twice Broken.*

Divorce is woven into the fabric of our culture. We can call out the names of divorced people, those whose paths we have crossed among family and friends, at our place of worship, or in the workplace. Blended families are no longer the exception, and shuttling children between households is a challenge common to many.

Familiarity, however, does not lessen anguish. For many people, the experience of divorce ushers in an extended period of grief, just as other life-altering losses do.

I am not a psychologist or a grief counselor, nor have I conducted research that will revolutionize the well-documented stages of grief. What I can offer is a glimpse into the very raw emotions that come from personal experience.

Initially I intended to portray grief in a generic light. Over time I recognized how impossible that would be. Grief is a personal story that is best told in the context of real life. Eventually I conceded. The first two chapters of *Twice Broken* relate those circumstances that led me into the tunnel of grief.

The chapter "Broken in Body" is the story of an early marriage that was strained and eventually devastated by pornography, physical abuse, and emotional abandonment. In its draft form, "Broken in Body" was an emotionless, vague story told from thirty thousand feet. I did not remember much of my life between the ages of eighteen and twenty-four, or maybe I did not want to remember.

Little by little, I zeroed in on a few particular memories in hopes of providing insight into the reality of domestic violence. There is much more that could be said, but no amount of graphic detail will add to the message of *Twice Broken*, a message of hope and the new life that does exist beyond the tunnel of grief.

Chapter two, "Broken in Spirit," considers the repercussions of abuse, the pain of infidelity, and the shame of a second divorce. It also touches on the challenges of forging a new life as a middle-aged woman.

My zero-for-two marital track record is not the legacy I had hoped would be recorded in my family genealogy for generations to come. If my first divorce was a scarlet badge of shame, my second was a pronouncement of utter worthlessness. The saving grace of my second divorce was the patient acceptance I received from those closest to me. That support system is an important part of the story I want to share.

At the end of each chapter, a "Letter to Liv" has been added to honor the kind and wise actions of those who stood by me as I stepped out from under the cloak of marriage and back into the world of a single woman.

At some point, you will likely find yourself walking beside a friend, a family member, or a coworker who is struggling through grief, perhaps as a result of emotional abandonment, physical abuse, or divorce. You might be the only constant when her life is crumbling, and your compassion and steadfastness will be important stepping stones along her path to healing. You are *Liv*.

What a challenging role to play. You might come alongside her while she is bound in a detrimental relationship or trapped in a place of continued denial. You might find her wallowing in self-pity or caught in the grip of bitterness, perhaps because of a relationship that ended months or even years before. You have listened, consoled, and encouraged. Time has passed, but nothing has changed.

For you, *Twice Broken* is a lens that peers into the tunnel of suffering, that dark place through which some pass and others stay.

My hope is that by seeing what your loved one sees, you might become better equipped to respond to her changing needs. Each "Letter to Liv" shares a bit of quiet advice that might be useful to you as you share her journey.

Perhaps you are the one who is walking (or crawling) through a place of brokenness. You don't need to be told what the tunnel is like, because you live there. *Twice Broken* is not a remedy for your pain or a secret that will hasten your journey. For you, it is an affirmation that the swinging pendulum of your emotions is normal.

It is a reminder to lean when you are too weak to stand. It is a message of hope that you cannot yet imagine for yourself.

The story of *Twice Broken* begins at brokenness, but it ends at a place of wholeness. Let's walk together toward that place of healing.

Prologue

Your desire shall be to thy husband.
Genesis 3:16

Broken in Body

A bruised reed he will not break,
and a smoldering wick he will not snuff out.
In faithfulness, he will bring forth justice.
Isaiah 42:3

He jerked his wrist clockwise, pulling taut the handful of hair already entwined in his fingers. My head snapped back, and I had no choice but to look up at him. His tall frame towered beside my kneeling one, and he glowered down at me with disdain.

With his left hand he lifted a round and ripened peach for me to see, pausing long enough to bask in my mounting fear. In a calculated manner he brought the peach to his mouth and took one large bite and then another.

He turned what remained of the peach in his hand, confirming that the jagged pit had been exposed. Placing the pit against the right side of my face, he dragged it methodically and repeatedly in an up and down motion. I could not suppress a quiet gasp of pain.

When he was satisfied with his show of dominance, he released my hair and gave me a quick shove backward. I remained breathless and still, counting each subtle creak as his weight shifted on the steps leading from the basement to the living area.

Nine, ten, eleven, twelve. I heard the door at the top of the stairs open, and I waited for the click of the latch as the door settled back into place. Only then did I get to my feet.

I raised my hand, gingerly cupping the right side of my face, hoping to keep the blood from dripping onto the floor. Its stickiness was drying between my fingers by the time I reached the bathroom. I grabbed the white hand towel and dabbed gently at the blood. Turning my head slightly to the left, I leaned closer to the mirror. My mind was already evaluating the best response to anyone who might ask about the slashes that began at my cheekbone and followed the downward contour of my face.

After a minute or two, I shoved the stained towel securely inside my sweater, held my head up, and walked back into the sickening masquerade of contentment.

I did not run, because I was afraid.

Only years later did I understand how effectively Adam had used fear to control me. It had been his tool from the beginning, his way of conditioning and manipulating me.

My first lesson was quickly learned. Pain would always follow anger. Because I could not foresee all the things that would trigger Adam's anger, I kept peace at all costs. My words were carefully measured, and my emotions remained my own. I cowered when I should have stood. I learned to dread his footsteps in the hall, the turn of a door handle, menacing looks, and a heartless touch.

Adam and I began dating when we were both sixteen. He was the star halfback on the high-school football team. He bench-pressed more than most, and he ran faster than all the rest. It was exhilarating to know that he was attracted to me when so many other girls were competing for his attention.

Our first interaction was an understated, parking-lot invitation to the fall homecoming dance. I was drawn by his shy ways and his unexpectedly quiet demeanor. As we began to date regularly, I found that he was more interested in healthy eating habits than weekend drinking parties. He took me to romantic restaurants. He opened my car door, and sometimes he had a bag of my favorite candy waiting for me on the car seat. A friend once commented that he cared for me as gently as one might care for a delicate china doll.

By the time we graduated from high school, we had been dating for two years. When Fall rolled around, I stayed on the East Coast to study at a local community college. Adam headed to the Midwest to play football at the college of his dreams. We transitioned to a long-distance relationship, talking by phone, writing letters, and spending school breaks together.

The mechanics of the relationship kept working, but the dynamics were shifting. Adam was living in an expanded world and creating a network of new relationships. I, on the other hand, found few friends among the meager number of commuting students. Instead of finding new ways to fill the void, I held tightly to the relationship I knew best.

By the end of our first semester, Adam was talking about marriage. My will began to buckle under his persistence, and I was too immature to realize that I was already engaged in a controlling relationship. By summer I had traded my dream of true love for the habit of emotional dependency.

We married in mid-July, in a small church filled with solemn family members and friends who privately surmised that I was pregnant.

In early August, we loaded a trailer with secondhand furniture and drove more than one thousand miles to our first home, a tiny efficiency apartment equipped with undersized appliances and an abundance of cockroaches. Adam's summer was filled with long football practice sessions, so I spent those first days on my own, learning to drive a stick shift through a maze of one-way city streets. Soon it was time for us to begin fall classes.

It's doubtful that any eighteen-year-old knows what to expect from marriage, but my heart and mind were uneasy from the start. Adam had a dark, vindictive nature that began to exert itself in every aspect of our new life together. I worked diligently to maintain an environment free of conflict, always fearful of tipping the unspoken balance.

Before we had been married for one month, Adam led me to a stash of boxes that he had kept hidden from me. He opened the first box and pulled out what seemed to be a treasured belonging. When he turned toward me, I saw that he was holding a pornographic magazine. The box behind him was filled with two neat stacks of magazines, and I assumed that each of the other boxes held the same. Adam's implication was clear, and before long it became a direct challenge: Why couldn't I look and act like these women? I tried, but it was never enough.

A seed of doubt began to grow inside of me, self-doubt. I had competition, and I learned to fear my inability to compete with the flawless beauties who had captured Adam's attention. They had faces and names, and to me they were very real intruders in my marriage.

Adam vowed to put aside what seemed to be a growing obsession. Despite his repeated promises, however, I continued to find evidence of his pervasive habit. I fell into a compulsive pattern of searching the apartment, and I always found something. I believe Adam wanted it that way. It was a mind game, and I had lost what turned out to be one of many battles for control.

Three months into our fledgling marriage, I lost another battle. Adam was resting on the bed when I leaned playfully forward to talk to him. His arms were crossed casually across his chest. Without warning or provocation, he swung his left arm at me with great force. I heard the dull thud and felt the crackling pain as his closed fist connected with my jaw.

For a brief moment I couldn't absorb the reality of the situation. Finally, stunned and angry, I stormed out of the apartment and jumped into the car. I had no intention of tolerating physical abuse. Before long, my anger gave way to hurt and disbelief. How could my own husband treat me this way? What could I have done to trigger such a violent reaction?

I drove down the few city streets that were familiar to me, trying to come up with some plan of action. I had no friends or family in the area, and I had no money. By 1:00 a.m. my resolve had begun to falter. I swallowed my pride and returned to the apartment to confront Adam. He immediately discounted my version of the story, claiming he had no memory of hitting me. Most likely, he concluded, he had been asleep and therefore was not accountable for his actions. In that moment I found it easier to accept his lie than to face the truth. It was a disastrous choice.

A pattern of abuse quickly emerged. If I did not behave as Adam thought I should, his first response was physical aggression. Sometimes he would throw me to the floor or shove me across the room. Other times he vented his rage by repeatedly banging my head against the wall. At first I tried to fight back, but I was no match for his strength. Before long, the physical violence became an almost daily occurrence. By the time we reached our first anniversary, I had begun to fear for my life.

Kathleen Serenko

One particular evening, Adam became angry because I talked to him while he was watching television. In frustration I snapped a comment in his direction and headed toward the bedroom. He was on his feet immediately, chasing me down the hall. I felt his hands dig into my shoulders, and he spun me around to face him. With one push he hurled me several feet backward onto the bed. When I tried to sit up, he pushed me down again. Then he climbed above me, straddled my body, and used his knees to pin my arms to the bed. His weight settled on my chest.

I threw my body upward in a frantic and repeated effort to free myself. My struggle seemed to amuse him, but only for a moment. He wrapped his hands around my neck and pressed his thumbs against my airway. My eyes fixated on his, searching for some sign of compassion or regret. I saw none. Instead, he tightened his grip until I could no longer breathe. I'm not sure how long he held me there, savoring his role as tormentor, but it was long enough to intensify the fear that already ruled my life.

When he finally released me, I fled the apartment, his verbal insults trailing behind. By that time I had developed a few friendships from school. I drove in blind fear to one classmate's apartment. I sat in her tiny living room, visibly shaken, yet pretending as if I had stopped by for a casual visit. I never breathed a word about the abuse. Instead I gave some lame excuse for the striations that marked my throat. I doubt my story was believable.

I sustained other injuries throughout the years, but the abuse remained our little secret. To the outside world, Adam was quiet and unassuming, a university football player worthy of special attention. No one ever knew when my ribs were cracked by a heavy boot hurled in anger. No one saw the shoe-print bruise that darkened the inside of my thigh. No one ever felt the tender welts hidden so often beneath my long hair.

After every instance of physical aggression, Adam would leave the apartment. I never knew where he went or how long he would be gone. This repetitive abandonment became very traumatic for me.

On one particularly cold winter night, Adam left me alone. I felt I would suffocate if I did not escape the silence and rejection of the empty apartment. I donned a warm coat and headed outside, curling up under the branches of a large shrub at one entrance of our apartment complex. I anxiously scanned each passing vehicle, wanting him to return, yet fearing his presence. After several hours I pulled my frigid body from concealment and went back into the apartment. Adam had not yet returned. He never knew that I had waited so long in the cold, nor would he have cared.

Physical abuse is frightening and demeaning. It leaves wounds that take time to heal and scars that never go away. The same can be said of emotional abuse.

The prevailing solution offered to women trapped in physically and emotionally abusive relationships is simple: "Just leave!" Unfortunately, that advice is not as easy to follow as it is to give.

The psyche of an abused person is a challenge to understand. Even the victim is ill-equipped to identify the factors that keep her bound: fear, false guilt, a lack of identity, confusion, the desire to be loved, or simply a place to live. Every situation is different, but there are common threads that help explain why some victims remain in dangerous relationships.

Emotional and physical abuse are forms of erosion. They wear away all that is healthy. Sometimes the erosion comes swiftly and dislodges great chunks of confidence. Other times it slowly chips away at self-esteem and emotional health. Eventually the victim's sense of identity has been washed away, and a layer of confusion is all that remains. She has been transformed from an independent person with original thoughts and strong passions into a passive, emotionally dependent shadow of her former self. Without the approval of her abuser, she has no worth.

Disapproval can be communicated in a number of ways. For example, a dog that has just chewed a favorite pair of shoes might be scolded with a sharp tone or some physical gesture that says, "Bad dog!" He will cower in shame for a moment and then come back with exaggerated affection in an effort to regain approval.

An abused woman responds in a similar manner. She has been blamed, berated, and belittled. She has begun to believe that she is a "bad dog," and nothing she does is good enough to win the approval of her abuser. Still, she tries.

Adam was always attracted to a quick moneymaking scheme, and one fleeting idea was to breed and sell Doberman Pinschers. We were apartment dwellers, so the dogs resided at a friend's house, often in the basement because of the harsh midwestern winters. Each night a terrible mess littered the basement floor. Adam demanded that I handle the daily cleanup.

I was getting ready to leave for a required class activity one evening when he insisted that I first clean the basement. When I objected, he pushed me back and began to slam my head against the wall, stopping only when my will caved to his. He drove me to the friend's house, and I hurried to clean the dogs' urine and feces from the floor, trying hard to regain my composure as I worked. Even in that filthy basement, I was the bad dog.

When I finished cleaning, I headed to a local health fair to conduct hearing screenings as part of my class requirement. I arrived late, but no one seemed to notice. I longed for one of my classmates to see something amiss in my eyes, to hear my silent plea for help. If one did recognize my pain, I could not tell.

I wonder now how I could have been so passive. I had allowed Adam to determine my worth. His judgment had become my truth, and I had relinquished the power of decision in my own life. Instead of taking action, I waited for someone to see my heartache and act on my behalf. I waited, but that day never came.

Why, like so many other victims of domestic violence, did I remain silent? The easy answer is shame. The one who had promised to love me most had judged me worthless. I was unlovable. To hide my shame, I created a decorative wall for others to see. I hid my bruises, and I denied the abuse. Once this pattern of abuse and protective silence had been established, it was not easily broken.

During those years I had a part-time job cleaning the home of Miss Elizabeth, an elderly widow whose most treasured family member was a little Pomeranian named Foxy. When Miss Elizabeth was out of town, I kept an eye on Foxy. One night, when I couldn't take any more of Adam's abuse, I slipped away to find refuge with Foxy.

After two nights, and before Miss Elizabeth returned, I went back to our apartment. Adam's mother phoned me later that day, and I knew immediately that Adam had gone before me, paving the way with another layer of deceit.

"Why," she challenged, "do you keep leaving him?"

It was my time. The invitation I had been waiting for had finally come. "Because I'm tired of being hit!" The truth hung in silence for a moment. Then, the unexpected.

"You must do something to make him hit you."

There it was. I was the bad one after all. Given my fragile state of mind, it took only one word of condemnation to drive me back into the silence of that unhealthy cycle. I did not discuss the abuse again, and Adam's mother never asked.

My next hope of freedom came a summer later when Adam and I traveled to see two of my brothers who were living in California. It was a clear and beautifully warm afternoon when we arrived at a local Mexican restaurant where we had agreed to meet. In my excitement, I was less careful than usual. It was only minutes before my older brother noticed a large and yellowing bruise on my left forearm. His question

to Adam barely masked a hint of aggression. I quickly
stepped in to absorb the blame: "I tripped and fell back
onto the television stand." The excuse came so easily.
After all, the bruise had formed when I fell onto the
television stand. I had simply substituted the words, *I
tripped*, for the more accurate, *Adam pushed me.* I was
so well trained by then.

After an awkward evening together, we all
headed to bed around eleven o'clock. By midnight,
Adam insisted that we make a clandestine departure
and drive hundreds of miles back toward our home.
For the first time, I felt safe in refusing him. I had a
place to stay and a resolve I had never before
possessed. He became irate and physically abusive,
and then he got in the car and drove away. I felt free.
For the first time, I did not chase after him with my tail
between my legs, begging for restored affection.

I stood alone in the living room, staring out
into the dark and starry sky. A key turned inside of my
heart, unlocking desires and the potential of an unseen
world. In that moment I made the decision to live life
my way.

After a few weeks in California, I flew to
Virginia to spend a month with my oldest brother and
his family. I went to cookouts and softball games, and
I held hands with a guy named Whitey, because I
could. I reconnected with my elementary-school
sweetheart, who also lived in the area. We skipped

rocks and talked, and I spent a night or two at his apartment, because I could. I was twenty years old, and for the first time, I felt my age.

From Virginia, I landed back in my hometown, where I stayed with another of my brothers and his family. There I reconnected with some high-school classmates. Together we crossed the state border and took advantage of the lower legal drinking age at a dive bar. I drank too much and I flirted, because I could.

Somewhere over the course of those two months, Adam tired of his new adventures and decided he was ready to regain control. He sent flowers. Next, a beautiful dress and then jewelry. Other gifts kept coming, but I felt bolder every time I rejected his overtures. Removed from his influence and exposed to the healthy logic of others, I had the strength to stay away. Still, a sickening feeling of dread always followed just one step behind.

As summer came to a close, I faced a challenging decision. I could transfer to another university and deal with a delay in graduation, or I could return to my existing college where I needed only a handful of credits to complete my degree. I thought I was strong enough to avoid Adam for one semester.

My family began to build a circle of protection around me, telling others that I had transferred to a different university. In the meantime, I quietly returned to finish my final semester of college. With more than thirty thousand students on campus, I thought I could remain undetected. Unfortunately, I had again underestimated Adam's punishing nature. He found me almost immediately and appeared everywhere I went. His wraithlike presence frightened me.

The choices I'd made throughout the summer began to trouble my conscience. Before long a dark cloud of self-condemnation descended, and my willpower faltered. Without the safety nets of a healthy environment and the sound logic of others, I had no one to keep me from falling.

In a moment of weakness, I allowed Adam to get close enough to talk to me. Somehow he convinced me to go with him to our old apartment. When I walked through that door, I stepped back into the tightly fenced world of doubts and fears. Adam had been watching for an opening, and he saw it in that moment. He zeroed in on my heart, conjuring up what seemed like heartfelt regret and sincere repentance. I had been desperate for his love for so long that I was willing to reach out and accept whatever morsel I could grasp. I forgave him.

The moment Adam regained his advantage, he took steps to cut me off from all outside connections. I was isolated from family, and one by one my friendships slipped away. Adam's foreboding demeanor and heartless comments reminded me that he had the power to take my life at any time. Fear was enough to keep me in line.

Ten months later, my first son was born. He had an easy smile, deep dimples, and more than enough energy. He was a ray of sunshine in a very dark existence.

Somehow in the midst of all the chaos, Adam and I earned our college degrees. He secured a promising career, and I dared to hope that we were finally on our way to a brighter future. He must have realized that his new career in federal law enforcement might be jeopardized, because the physical violence vanished in what would become our final year of marriage.

It wasn't long, however, before his cruelty surfaced in other ways. For months he had been baiting me with hints, mysterious phone calls, and sudden overnight assignments. He taunted me when I could not decipher his riddles. After he grew tired of that game, he laid it all out for me to see. Her name was Rachel, and he had been seeing her for months. He loved her, he said.

Less than one year after moving us to one of the country's largest cities, Adam disappeared from our lives. I was seven months pregnant, and our first son was just two years old. I was tired, and I was broken. I had no desire to fight for what should have been mine. I allowed him to terminate the marriage on his terms, with no commitment to child support or any other financial backing. I was determined to raise my two sons without being reliant on someone who had tossed me aside like the proverbial old shoe.

I never missed him, but he had left behind a very broken woman. For six years my focus had been on survival. My supply of hope, strength, and confidence had been depleted, but I never considered counseling or any other form of emotional support. In fact, I never discussed the abuse with anyone. It was behind me, and my life was busy. That shameful part of my past could stay hidden, I hoped.

My new survival consisted of earning an income and caring for my two young boys. I had options that would have allowed me to close the thousand-mile gap that separated me from family, but I chose to remain in my new surroundings. In hindsight, I can only guess that my mind was simply unable to cope with another new start.

It took time to press through the tunnel of grief, but I managed. I began to embrace my independence, and I grew stronger day by day. Hope returned, and I realized that life was not over after all. Though I craved a relationship, my heart was too raw and my life was too busy. I also doubted that I could ever trust a man.

Only one thing was certain; I never again wanted to experience such brokenness.

Broken in Spirit

The LORD is close to the brokenhearted
and saves those who are crushed in spirit.
Psalm 34:18

He told me I was beautiful.

Until that time I had viewed all men as a collective enemy. It's not that I didn't long for a relationship, because I did. My four years as a single mother were filled with many lonely, sleepless nights. There were times when I wept silently at the sight of a man draping his arm gently across the shoulder of his wife. My heart was heavy when I saw a father playing catch with his son or teaching him to ride a bike. Sometimes I just wanted someone with me when I carried the groceries, cradled a sick child, filled the gas tank, or came home at the end of a long day.

I had foolishly wasted my one golden ticket to a happy marriage, or so I thought. I was a twenty-four-year-old divorced mother of two very young boys. I couldn't imagine men lining up to learn more about that opportunity.

Besides, the attention of a man made me uncomfortable. I averted my eyes whenever I could. I never initiated a conversation. If I did have to communicate, I maintained a distant posture and kept the interaction as brief as possible. When a coworker made an overture, I had a ready excuse.

I was also a man hater. It sounds incongruous to be afraid of men and to hate them at the same time, but the two attitudes did coexist in my life. A real man, in real flesh, in the real world made me nervous. The men in my mind made me angry. They were the ones who had their noses buried in porn magazines at local convenience stores. They parked their trucks at strip joints, and they lied to their wives. They spent their family's money on other women, and they made off with the hopes and dreams of their wives. I despised them all, and it was because of them that I kept myself safely tucked behind a wall of stoicism.

After four years, I was desperate to venture beyond that wall. I was looking for an imaginary man, the knight in shining armor who would love me forever. Rick was the first to come along.

Given the disaster of my first marriage, it would seem logical that I would have carefully evaluated the next man who crossed my path, vetting him according to a lengthy list of requirements. My logic, however, was still faulty. Rather than judging the man, I continued to judge myself. It would be my good fortune, I thought, if any man looked my way.

I knew from the beginning of my relationship with Rick that I was making a sacrifice. I was not physically attracted to him, and we had few mutual interests. His parenting skills were also untested, but he offered what I needed most at that time: he did not bang my head against the wall, he used words of affirmation, and he promised to love my boys as his own. It was enough. We married after a short courtship.

I believed that I had made a wise long-term investment. I was sure Rick would always be loyal to me and kind to my boys. Nothing was more important.

After a brief honeymoon we returned to my apartment, which would be our new home as a married couple. A sinking feeling followed me through the front door: *he was here to stay*. The gravity of my rushed decision was immediately clear. Once again I had stepped into less than best.

Rick was consistently affectionate, and that was a breath of fresh air. He was never violent or verbally abusive to me, but I did recognize that he was very immature and sometimes much too harsh when he interacted with my sons. I chocked that up to a lack of parenting experience, and I was confident that he would adjust his approach along the way. Unfortunately, I was blind to the strong undercurrents that would one day erupt in the most damaging of ways.

Despite some of the usual family problems, our first two years of marriage passed rather uneventfully. Our relationship was fairly strong at the start of year three when a beautiful little girl came our way. Rick doted on her, and she had two adoring big brothers.

At times my trust in Rick faltered, and I would imagine the possibility of infidelity. A gut feeling here, a bad dream there. Explanations that seemed implausible: the aroma of perfume, Rick's frantic behavior when he forgot his phone at home, new hobbies, new clothing, and more side jobs. When I questioned a circumstance or conveyed a concern, Rick was quick to blame my insecurities. I would chastise myself, knowing he must be right. It could never happen twice.

As time passed, the turmoil continued to stir inside of me despite Rick's reassurances. Was I transferring my old fears into this new relationship? Was I unfairly holding Rick accountable for the hurts Adam had inflicted? Or was my heart revealing truths I did not want to accept? I didn't have the answers to my own questions.

At times I was overcome by old and compulsive behaviors. Every time I searched Rick's car, his wallet, the closet, or his briefcase, I had a sick sense that I would find something incriminating. I always hoped otherwise, but one day my hopes were dashed.

On my daughter's second birthday, I learned about "her."

It was 10:00 a.m., and I was on my third load of laundry. Saturdays had fallen into a deep rut of housework, lawn work, and grocery shopping. As usual, Rick was sleeping late, but it didn't matter. My list of chores would have been the same regardless. The only difference on this day was that I also needed to prepare for a birthday party.

With every step I took, nagging thoughts followed. I justified a quick search to allay my fears, hoping I would be able to shed the burden of worry. After stuffing a load of towels into the washer, I closed the lid and headed to the kitchen where I knew I would find Rick's truck keys.

The humidity was stifling that August morning, but that was typical for our city and others along the Gulf Coast. My heart was beating quickly, but I walked nonchalantly to the driver's-side door of the truck, aware that a neighbor could be watching. The ten-year-old truck was well past its prime, but Rick had insisted on adding a lift kit. I swung open the heavy door and hopped up onto the threshold. I felt an overwhelming sense of dread as I slid into the worn leather seat. For a few seconds I remained completely still, wavering between the desire to trust and the compulsion to search. Compulsion won.

I opened the glove compartment, rifled through a disorganized stack of papers, and carefully checked inside the tight vinyl cover of the owner's manual. Nothing. I glanced nervously toward the front door of the house, hoping that Rick was still asleep. Next I reached under the driver's seat, feeling blindly for any bit of evidence that might have been left behind. I leaned head first toward the passenger side and slipped my left arm under that seat as well. Nothing there, and nothing above the visors.

I shifted slightly in the driver's seat to find a convenient angle, and I lifted the cover of the middle console. What remained of my trust was shattered in that instant. I could not look away from the box of condoms and the pink lined paper that recorded her name, address, and phone number. I felt shock, devastation, and anger, in that order.

I yanked up on the handle and threw the truck door open, content to know that I had caused it to rock violently on its hinges. I jumped to the ground and threw the door back into place with all my might. I wanted the world to know that I was angry.

I barreled through the front door of the house and down the hall toward our bedroom, sidestepping another pile of laundry along the way. I had no conscious thoughts. I simply followed rage where it led me.

Rick must have heard me coming. He was standing beside the bed, hastily buttoning his jeans by the time I stepped into the room. I hurled the box of condoms at him and rushed forward, my arms swinging. I had every intention of hitting him, but he threw up his left arm to block me. The crook of a broken finger reminds me still of that ugly day.

I can't recall what happened between the first moment of confrontation and the time Rick headed out of the house with a black trash bag stuffed with his belongings. I don't know if he packed it, or if I did.

I listened until I heard the front door slam shut and then the rough idle of the truck as it started down the road.

He was gone, and my rage was spent. I sat on the edge of the bed, trying to absorb anything that would make sense. Nothing did. I crumbled to my knees, pressed my face against the mattress, and I cried.

Pain that begins in the soul cries differently than the pain of injury or the sadness of a bad day. It begins in the deepest part of who we are, and it passes through every fiber of our being on its way to an outward display of grief. A soul cry comes in waves, it has no words, and it cannot be comforted.

The rest of the day and night was a blur. I don't know how long I remained on my knees. I don't remember if my kids were home, what they might have been doing, what they might have heard, or what they might have thought. Kids, I have come to realize, are the biggest losers when parents fail to keep their lives in order.

What I do remember is being called upon the next day to defend my actions. Rick's father was a pastor. In his need to spiritually assess the situation, he questioned whether my angry response was appropriate behavior for a Christian woman. The challenge was eerily familiar, and I didn't have the capacity to do anything other than doubt myself. As the years have passed, I've come to recognize an obvious truth: he had never looked into the face of an adulterous spouse.

By the next day, Rick had reopened communication. I should not have been surprised when he did what liars do best. He lied some more. I have no idea how he could deny such incriminating evidence, but he did. Even more disturbing was that I allowed him to adjust his story until it aligned with my emotions. When denial did not soothe me, he showed sorrow.

If only I had known then what I know now: a forgiving nature is an admirable trait, but forgiveness without accountability is weakness. I was weak.

Though my heart fought against it, I succumbed to Rick's words of reassurance. I simply could not accept that I had misjudged a second man. I had already failed at one marriage, and I could not risk failing again, no matter the cost.

In the sixth year of our marriage, another beautiful daughter was added to our family. By then life had settled into an extremely hectic pattern of career, housework, financial challenges, and child rearing. The strain increased as our children grew. Rick's facade as a patient father continued to crumble, and my sons became the primary targets of his rage. Because of my own emotional challenges and a misplaced loyalty to my marriage, I failed to act on their behalf as decisively as I should have. It is my greatest regret to this day.

Over the course of the next five years, my trust was continually tested. I never uncovered definitive proof of Rick's cheating, but the signs pointed in that direction many times over. It had become impossible for me to differentiate between unfounded fears and valid intuitions.

Who was Connie, and what did her cryptic note mean? Was the Christmas card from the apartment manager really a note of thanks, or did it have an underlying meaning? Why did his coworkers smirk when I joined him for lunch? Could the credit card statement really be wrong when it showed a charge for two movie tickets instead of one?

In the eleventh year of our marriage, I could no longer deny the obvious as it unfolded before me. The bright computer screen. The open porn site. The history of online searches, and the numerous personal connections. I was embarrassed, disgusted, and angry. I told Rick to get out, and I knew then that I did not want to reconcile.

I could not envision the restoration of a marriage so broken, nor could I imagine making a new life for myself and my kids. I had two teenage boys, two young daughters, one small income, and no savings.

After six months of separation, Rick asked me to attend counseling with him. I was so surprised by his willingness to come clean that I once again accepted his repentance as sincere. Facing the old demons of pornography, however, was an especially difficult process for me.

For years I have heard individuals debate the effects of pornography. Some say it is harmless, but I know differently. I resented these other women in my life, the ones who leered at me from the pages of magazines and the screens of Internet porn sites. These women with their seductive looks and the promise of providing my husband what he could never find in the restricting confines of a relationship with one woman. Promises that had nothing to do with love, but everything to do with imagination and self-driven pleasure. Women whose flawless beauty reminded me that with my average looks, I could never satisfy a man.

Where were these women, I wondered, when our family was in need? Did they spend a long night walking our fevered child or comforting our little girl when she cried out in fear? Did they grocery shop, cook, and clean when it should have been time to rest? Were they willing to sacrifice a manicure and a fashionable haircut so the kids could have lunch money? Did they select birthday presents with love or feel pride when a new art project came home from school?

Our marriage, or what was left of it, lasted another seven years. The chasm between Rick and the boys widened. I remained oblivious to the subtle and not-so-subtle signs of Rick's continued infidelity. My head was buried in the daily crush of life, and it remained there until I could bury it no more.

It was a mild April day, just two days before Easter, that day of the great divide. After a relatively mundane argument, Rick announced that he was leaving for good. I was confused and devastated. What about all the sacrifices I had made, all the time and energy I had invested? Had it all been a waste of time?

Rick pulled the girls aside. He spun his final story of family betrayal, explaining that an unhappy marriage wasn't a good thing. He comforted the girls by saying that he might return in a month or two, or maybe even later that night, and then he drove away.

I could not fathom the reason for his unexpected departure. My twenty-one-year-old son was not so naïve. He suggested that Rick might have a girlfriend. It was a logical assumption, but for some reason I was not equipped to accept it. When the cell phone bill arrived at the end of the month, a cursory view of the detailed calls supported my son's theory. Of course, Rick denied having an affair.

Here I pause to ask myself *why*? Why had I been so blind to what must have been so obvious to others? Why was I shocked? Why did I keep trying to find ways to bridge the gap between us?

Why did I choose to forgive yet again?

I was either remarkably devoted or fairly delusional, believing I had the power to keep my family together. My choice to reconcile was the first step in a gut-wrenching, intense commitment that would stretch over the next four months.

Rick claimed to extricate himself from the affair. As more details surfaced, I learned that he had been seeing this particular woman for nine months before he moved out of our house. The knowledge of this extended betrayal was painful and humiliating.

Some will say I was a fool to forgive or to consider trusting again, and they would probably be right. At the time it was a chance I was willing to take. If I had to walk through a second divorce, I wanted to know that I had done everything in my power to salvage my family. I know now that it was blind and misplaced devotion, but at the time it seemed a like a necessary step.

Rick and I committed to individual counseling, and then we began to attend counseling together. From all appearances, our marriage was one of the lucky few that would beat the odds. We were rebuilding what appeared to be a loving relationship over the shards of broken trust. Daily I battled hurtful reminders and tormenting thoughts. It was not an easy process, but we had support from family and friends. Each day, Rick spoke gentle words of love and affirmation. We made plans to renew our vows, and we even purchased new, symbolic rings to mark the occasion. At the first of August, he moved back into our home.

Less than four weeks had passed when I sensed another ominous shift. Rick had become restless and unsettled. By the end of August, he made a choice to walk away from me and back to his girlfriend. While I had been committed to forgiveness, I was not willing to remain as the last side of a twisted triangle. This, without question, was the end.

Over the years I had watched women struggle through divorce during their middle-aged years. It had always horrified me. Now here I was, facing a second divorce. Double heartache, double shame. I was reeling from broken trust, humiliation, shame, fear, and resentment. It was too much. There were times when I sat alone in my car or in my room and screamed, because a scream was all that would come.

I begged God to intervene, to spare me the pain and the grief. Sometimes, however, life leads us down a path not of our choosing. It became obvious that my children and I were going to experience the tragedy of a broken family for a second time.

Several factors intensified the pain of my second divorce. When I married Rick, I had invested in forever. I had counted on loyalty and kindness at the sacrifice of other pleasures. I had trusted him when I thought I could trust no one else.

He said he understood the devastation of my first divorce, yet he chose to send me down that same dark path again. Because of this, the wounds he inflicted were in some ways worse than those I had experienced from Adam's physical abuse.

I was twenty years older, making it a more daunting task to begin life anew. I faced more grave financial concerns, and I believed Rick had selfishly wasted my final opportunity for a happy marriage.

The shame of a second divorce was suffocating. Two men had tried me and pronounced me worthless. I was more convinced than ever that no man would ever want me.

Emotionally, I was a totally broken woman. Though I had navigated grief before, I could not comprehend ever walking away from this experience as a whole person.

In the pages that follow, I have tried to capture the excruciating journey through grief. Each chapter relates a single emotional response. Some came and went, brief flashes of agony. Others represent intense suffering that lingered for months. A few returned again and again, almost as a concerted effort to keep me down, to destroy me once and for all.

It is difficult to consider some of my experiences as they are written. It is difficult because I wonder how I could have remained blind to the truth of my situation. Why had I held onto another relationship that was so harmful? Why did I lack the strength to distance myself and my children from something so negative? Some of these answers would be uncovered only by making another long journey through grief.

Many of you will personally relate to the emotions presented here, because you know all too well the crushing pain of rejection and loss. I invite you to walk with me through the tunnel of grief and on to that place where brokenness becomes the gateway to wholeness.

Tunnel of Grief

Be merciful to me, O LORD,
for I am in distress;
my eyes grow weak with sorrow,
my soul and my body with grief.
My life is consumed by anguish
and my years by groaning;
my strength fails because of my affliction,
and my bones grow weak.
Psalm 31:9–10

Instantly Shattered

Suddenly shall calamity come;
suddenly shall you be broken without remedy.

Proverbs 6:15

The moment is forever etched into my memory. As Rick drove away from our home, I recognized the finality of it all. After eighteen years our marriage was over, and in this one painful, searing act my greatest fear became reality.

There is a cushion of God's design that protects us at the very moment of tragedy. Because I was overwhelmed with pain, I could not appreciate this protective shield that, for a bit, lessened the full force of my circumstance.

Body and mind ground to a halt, like a city in the wake of a power outage. Time froze. Thoughts became jumbled. Sleep evaded me, and my appetite disappeared. All of life now revolved around this one shattering event.

I was fixed in the moment, waiting for some semblance of normalcy to return. It was God's mercy that I could not foresee every emotion, every financial outcome, or every gut-wrenching conversation that would haunt me over the next weeks and months. I felt only the pain of the moment. Perhaps that was all I could manage.

Words do little to express the wild range of emotions that assailed me in those first hours. Uninvited thoughts ran rampant. They ushered in fear, resentment, shame, and despair, emotions that would hound me throughout the grieving process.

I was in a form of suspended existence, somewhere between the reality of the past and the unknown life that lay before me. Even as I struggled to make sense of the moment, my thoughts raced ahead to wrestle with what this might mean to my future. I began to evaluate the uncharted territory ahead of me. How would I manage? Could I afford the mortgage, or would I have to sell the house? Did this mean I would be alone forever?

I did not want to voice my new reality. To speak the words, "He left, and he's not coming back," might make them true. I walked through the neighborhood, mindlessly retracing steps down familiar streets. I continued to walk and to breathe, not because I chose to, but because they were the involuntary routines of life. I wandered aimlessly, hoping for a measure of distraction from the torment that was clawing at every recess of my mind. Eventually I managed to make one phone call to a close friend. "He's gone," were the only words I could utter.

It was happening. Despite my resistance, I was being thrust into the entrance of the long, dark tunnel of grief. I knew this place. I recognized the blackness in front of me, a shapeless void waiting to devour me.

It was as if my eyes, accustomed to bright sunlight, suddenly were immersed into total darkness. I could see nothing clearly, but I sensed the murky images and nameless forces that surrounded me. Fear took hold, but when I looked back, I saw no escape.

In that moment, I knew the only way out was to endure the long and agonizing journey before me. I could not fathom what might lie ahead, but I already knew I did not have the courage to face the decisions and heartache that lurked in the tunnel. I could not take even a single step forward.

All I could do was stand in that terrifying moment and become accustomed to the darkness.

Dear Liv,

Thanks for coming when I called tonight. I knew I could count on you, even though you're so busy with your own family.

I appreciate the time you spent with the girls. I didn't want them to see me like that, and it was so helpful that you kept them distracted. It was also a huge help that you fixed their dinner and made sure they were ready for bed. From one mom to another, nothing means more than having someone look out for your kids.

It meant a lot that you didn't sit around and criticize Rick, or tell me how much better off I'm going to be without him. It's probably true, but right now I can't feel glad that he's gone. All I can think of is what it's going to be like to be alone.

I felt safe calling you, because I knew you wouldn't expect me to explain. I don't even know myself what's happening or what

I'm going to do next. I don't even want to think about it right now.

I know I did nothing but cry all night, but you did a great job handing me tissues— all two boxes of them! Seriously, thanks for sitting beside me and allowing me to grieve.

Always,
Your friend in need

Give Me the Quick Fix

For my thoughts are not your thoughts,
neither are your ways my ways, saith the Lord.
Isaiah 55:8

My eyes were finally adjusting to the darkness of the tunnel. I was beginning not to accept, but at least to recognize the reality of my situation. I could think and feel nothing beyond my circumstance, and the injustice of it was maddening.

I am not certain if my reaction at this point was one of fear, pride, or simply the desire to control my little world. All I know is that I wanted a quick fix. I did not like the tunnel, and I had no intention of staying there. Penance, prayer, self-improvement—I was willing to do whatever it would take to make my world right.

I lifted my left hand toward the heavens and pushed forward my ring finger, intending to give God a better view. I reminded him of the rights I had purchased with my wedding band and marriage vows: a lifetime of fidelity, companionship, and happiness. I knew he wanted nothing less for me.

I took one bold step forward, convinced that there must be another way out. God could not expect me to endure another journey through such devastating grief. I quickly began to calculate the actions required to fix my marriage. I was good at formulating plans of action, and this would be no different. With some spiritual focus and a bit of sacrifice, I knew I could make this mess disappear. Why should I stand still in the darkness? It was time to get moving.

"Step back, God," I thought, "I can take it from here."

When Rick walked away, I was forty-five years old and the mother of four children. I was at my heaviest weight ever, and other natural signs of aging had begun. I worked late into the evening four nights each week, and I came home tired, typically lugging a stack of work along with me. Cooking, cleaning, homework duty, and every other household chore awaited me each night.

Now flip the coin. Rick had been romancing someone sixteen years younger than me. She had one school-aged child and no job. She lived under the roof of someone who provided for her. I imagine that she was always available when I was working, always energetic when I was tired, and always attentive when I was overwhelmed.

I had so much work to do to regain the ground that had once been mine. That's why I had to get moving. I had so many things to fix.

It is a dangerous juncture when we decide that God is not moving fast enough or in the direction of our choosing. We can wait on him, or we can begin to chart our own course and our own timeline. In my case, I wanted my marriage to survive. Who could argue against such a noble desire? By what means was I willing to salvage the relationship? This is the point where God and I might have parted paths.

There is a hint of perverse comedy to the picture I must have painted. Desperate to regain, retain, and deserve the love of my husband, I hurriedly plotted a frantic overhaul. I looked around me to gain some sense of what I was lacking. What had he found that I had failed to provide?

There is a culture craze, strong and prevalent, and it was waiting to suck me into its vacant ideals. It magnified each of my shortcomings and promised easy solutions. Even the grocery store checkout lane offered a plethora of expertise and much needed advice.

Hundreds of subtitles shouted out at me, telling me how to look sexy, smell sexy, walk sexy, and breathe sexy. Each week I hurried through the aisle, glancing with both disdain and curiosity at the feature articles that seemed to share a common theme, like "Fifteen New and Unbelievably Sexy Ways to Touch Your Man."

Then it came, that familiar self-doubt. What does *she* know that I don't know? What did *I* fail to do that would have made me more desirable or more lovable? What can *I* do now that will turn his attention back to me?

In my moment of desperation, I would have gone to any length to achieve what I perceived to be the greater good, saving my marriage. In hindsight, I imagine myself behaving as a trapped rodent, locked inside four walls of a glass cage, running headlong into each wall, never seeing the hopelessness of my efforts.

I was surrounded by unrealistic expectations and taunted by unattainable perfection. It was incredibly easy to identify my faults, and they were many. I created a to-do list that would quickly put everything back in order. It read like a last-minute holiday shopping list, overly aggressive, unrealistic, and certain to fall short of bringing full satisfaction. It went something like this:

I would get a gym membership to get my abs and stomach muscles as firm as possible, preferably within two to three weeks. Never mind that they had been stretched by four children and unexercised for twenty years. I could do it.

My pride (and my budget) would never allow for breast implants, but I could do isometric exercises. I read somewhere that only one thousand repetitions per day would result in a perceptible lifting effect. I could fit those in during my drive to work.

An appointment at the salon was a must. Manicure, pedicure, and waxing. Budget would have to take a backseat to beauty.

I was certain that my outdated hairstyle was another reason Rick had looked elsewhere. There had to be some new style that could make me look at least five years younger, and I would remember to get just a trim off of the length. Men prefer long hair.

I took one step after another toward the elusive goals of beauty and sex appeal, yet each time I walked past a mirror, the message was disturbing. The same middle-aged woman kept staring back at me. Her face was haggard and her body was nowhere close to fit.

I reminded myself of the goal. I knew this quick fix was going to cost me, but the effort would be rewarded when my husband looked at me with affection and desire. I pressed on.

Next was an inventory of my closet, and the news was not good. Too small, too tight, not right. Each piece of clothing brought the same distasteful response. I no longer owned a single piece of suitable clothing. I felt so ashamed when I realized that I was the reason his eyes had wandered. Once I lost the necessary weight, I would buy a completely new wardrobe.

I was going to have to jumpstart my weight loss though. I would fast for two or three weeks, drinking nothing but Ensure to keep my electrolytes in balance. I would see a new woman in the mirror in no time. Until then I would make a few minor style adjustments: booty-lifting jeans, push-up bras, and spandex bodysuits.

I would also pull my hemline up and my neckline down to show a little more skin. I realized I would also need to throw away all those sensible, comfortable shoes. It was time for sexy heels to show off my new pedicure.

I would make an appointment with a makeup expert. She could advise me on just the right skin-cleansing, age-defying, imperfection-covering formula. I would also take a few moments to learn some of those sultry eye-shadow techniques, so I could always have that inviting bedroom look.

So much to do, but at least now I knew what I needed to fix.

Even now I feel the need to stop and breathe. I was living in a panic-stricken state, rushing through life, my arms swinging wildly, grabbing up every supposed remedy offered by society. I was a rejected and abandoned woman, and I was sure that only unappealing, unattractive women were rejected. Sadly, I allowed false perceptions to continue to warp my already unhealthy self-image. In vain, I attempted any and every fix that caught my attention.

I suppose I shouldn't judge myself too harshly. God had, after all, gifted me with an innate nurturing tendency. I had spent a lifetime fixing things, making people happy, easing tension, pointing out a more efficient way to get things accomplished. I couldn't help that my family, friends, and coworkers didn't always accept the solutions I offered. God still appreciated my help. Didn't he?

It is amusing how I dictated solutions to God, professing my great faith in his wisdom, and then turning away when he failed to do things my way. While my heart's intent may have been to trust him, I mistakenly put my own plan of action into place.

The truth is, I would have done almost anything to "fix" my pain. Unfortunately, emotional turmoil had impaired my judgment. I had seen it happen to other women. I had watched them run into the arms of another man, seeking approval but finding humiliation. I had watched them fill their empty hearts with alcohol and prescription drugs. I knew that I, too, risked trading my conscience and character for the illusion of the quick fix, that appealing entrance to one more path of deception and disappointment.

The last thing I needed was to heap more personal regret on top of an already heavy burden of heartache. Though I was desperate for relief, I knew that I would eventually have to accept that there would be no quick fix, but only a very long and arduous journey through the tunnel ahead.

At this point in my journey I still believed I could single-handedly change my outcome. It was an act of unintentional self-deception, or perhaps it was simply an extension of the state of shock that had carried me to that point. It bought me a little more time. I was not yet ready to bear the full burden of the traumatic changes that awaited me. Mercifully, I could not yet see how very long and treacherous the tunnel of grief would be.

Dear Liv,

Everyone should have a friend like you.

I know you have your doubts about Rick and about our marriage, but you've been there for me anyway, every step of the way. I can tell that you're sad about the way he's treating me and the kids, but not once have you discouraged my dream of keeping my family together. You pray my prayers with me.

The whole thing is so humiliating, Liv. I'm tired of hearing people tell me what they think. They all shake their heads. Some tell me how surprised they are, while others insist they saw it coming. Do they ever consider that maybe I don't want to know what they think? That maybe I don't want to be the topic around their dinner table?

Thank goodness I have you. I can share anything, and I know it won't reach the end of the prayer chain before I finish saying it. Ha!

People seem to think they have my problems figured out, when I don't have them figured out myself! They want to give me advice about how I should or shouldn't feel, about what I should or shouldn't do. They act like they know Rick better than I do. You're one of the few who understands why I want to forgive him, even if he doesn't deserve it.

And one more thing...what other friend would bring me chocolate and coffee at midnight when I needed it most! I'm running around like a mad woman, trying to piece my life back together, and you're always doing something sweet, looking out for me. Like you always tell me, It's okay to laugh in the middle of pain.

I love that about you, Liv.

Still holding on,
Your friend in need

If Only

Who will bring any charge against those whom God has chosen? It is God who justifies.
Romans 8:33

The fuel that had been driving my quick-fix plan was running on empty. I still felt responsible for fixing my marriage, but I no longer had the emotional energy to execute my lofty plan. I began to look inward, searching for the errant behavior that had caused *me* to destroy my own marriage. I thought I could find the one reason that would explain why.

Why had this happened? Why me? Why now? A destructive seed of undeserved guilt took root, and its growth began to entangle my heart and mind. I had no defense against it. I knew all the right platitudes. God loved me. My children loved me. I had the love and respect of others. None of that knowledge, however, could replace the love and affection that my own husband had stripped from me. Why? What was wrong with me?

The cycle of self-inventory became a consuming and destructive force, a revolving door of inspection, finger-pointing, and guilt. The conclusion was always the same: "If only I had…"

If only I had shown more respect, given more affection, and loved more perfectly. If only I had paid more attention to my appearance and been more interesting. If only I had not been so critical, nagged so much about saving money, or complained about the dirty laundry. If only I.

I have looked down my spiritual nose at the self-inflicted beatings embraced by some religions, yet

I have engaged in a similar behavior. I never used whips or switches. My instruments of pain were the thoughts that cut, bruised, and helped destroy my own self-image. In essence, I wallowed in self-hatred even as I professed to be made in the image of a holy God.

I mistakenly, and perhaps arrogantly, assumed that my actions were the reason for the choices of others. My misguided assumptions resulted in untold hours of heartache and self-recrimination. They held me bound in a harmful relationship, loyal to a hope that had long been dead, searching for an answer that would never be found.

I circled back again and again to this portion of the tunnel. I returned even when I knew the decisions that had devastated my marriage were not my own. The guilt continued to stir within me. Rick's choices had to be a result of my failures, but I still could not determine what those failures were.

Only in hindsight did I understand the truth. I had allowed Rick's judgment to become my reality. Because he did not love me, I was unworthy of love. Because he rejected me, I had no intrinsic value. Based on this belief system, I naturally concluded that I was abandoned because I had nothing worthwhile to offer.

At this point in my journey, it was impossible for me to distinguish where I was in the tunnel of grief. The initial shock had passed, and the numbness had dissipated. I had come to the realization that there was no quick fix. I was beginning to shoulder the full brunt of reality, and a heavy cloak of despair had begun to settle. It was dark, and that was all I knew.

Dear Liv,

This is more than I can take. I'm not trying to be dramatic—I really mean it. It feels like my heart has been ripped open, and every bit of it has been shredded. I thought it would hurt less over time, but now I'm not so sure.

When I'm around you (and you are the best, by the way) or other people, it's a little easier—for a while. But sometimes, when I'm alone, I curl up on the floor of my room and cry out to God, "Help me! Help me!" I don't know what else to say.

I appreciate the way you are always there to encourage me, telling me that Rick is the loser and not me. And I know you mean it when you tell me that I'm pretty or better than that. I appreciate it, Liv, but I really don't believe those things about myself, not anymore.

It just seems like I've lost everything. I realize I'm not the only one who has suffered, but you know, sometimes I don't care—no matter how selfish that sounds. This is my pain, and I can't get away from it.

Your husband must be tired of seeing my number pop up on your phone. I feel bad relying on you so much, but you have a way of helping me get past those desperate times when I don't know what else to do.

I would be lying if I said that I feel God's love right now. I do have doubts, Liv, but I appreciate that you have enough faith to believe for the both of us.

What a friend you are, listening to me and accepting all of my lousy weaknesses. I'm sure I'll pull out of this eventually, and I know you will be happy when I do. Then maybe having coffee with me won't be nearly as depressing as it was the other day.

Love,
Your someday-less-depressing friend

Kicked to the Curb

The LORD will call you back as if you were
a wife deserted and distressed in spirit,
a wife who married young,
only to be rejected, says your God.
For a brief moment I abandoned you, but
with deep compassion I will bring you back.
Isaiah 54:6–7

Darkness now permeated my life. I was surrounded by an impenetrable wall that kept me from seeing or believing in a future that might exist beyond its limits.

I fumbled through life, trudging here, trudging there, and back again. My thoughts were tangled, but my emotions were not. They were excruciatingly clear, and I could find no relief from the sharp reality that tore at my heart.

I was now in the longest and darkest stretch of the tunnel. Reality had forcibly settled upon me. I was no longer in the protected place of denial, and there was no value in bargaining. The demise of my marriage was certain. This, I believed, was my new existence. I was doomed to remain in a place of acute awareness and unrelenting pain, powerless to dislodge its darkness.

Rick worked the day shift during the last ten years of our marriage, so he had always been home by late afternoon when the girls got back from school. It wasn't long, though, before he stopped returning to the house after work. My job required evening hours, but I couldn't bear seeing the girls absorb any more changes than they already had. Rather than leave them alone every afternoon and evening, I resigned. My income was gone, and Rick was withholding all financial support, content to fight that out in court when the time came. I didn't have any money to bridge the gap.

Foreclosure was imminent unless I could sell the house quickly. That uncertainty, along with the loss of safety nets like health insurance and a secure retirement, added to my burden.

I set to work preparing the house to be put on the market, but the repairs were absorbing most of the money I did have. Just two months later, I was hardly concerned about repairs. I had more immediate needs, like money to buy groceries.

That October was a very challenging month, but two unexpected kindnesses reminded me, at least momentarily, that I was not making the journey alone. The first was a gift of $500 from an aunt I hadn't seen in seven years. To my knowledge, she was not aware of my situation.

The second were the pizzas that faithfully awaited us each morning when we opened the refrigerator. They provided lunch and dinner, but more importantly they brought a smile to our faces each day. I was so thankful for my son who worked the night shift at a local pizzeria. His desire to care for his sisters and me is still one of the sweetest memories from those otherwise dark days.

I knew, however, that we could not remain in such a tenuous financial position. While I was confident that I would eventually find a job with more standard hours, I wasn't certain whether I could survive financially until then.

I began to consider a move back to my hometown where my family network would be much stronger. The decision would require a move across the country, and my girls would have to transfer to a new school district midway through the seventh and tenth grades. It also meant that I would be leaving my young-adult sons behind.

How, I wondered, could I possibly hold everything together? I felt ill-equipped to be an effective mother when I was struggling so much with my own problems.

Perhaps most painful during this time was the loss of relationship. I was making one decision after another, and I was doing it alone. I struggled with the agonizing realization that I might never be held again, that I might never enjoy the touch of a man's strong hand on mine or know the intimacy of marriage. I might never again be the most important person in someone else's life. These were crushing losses that others around me were less likely to recognize, and I did not voice them. It was much safer to share about finances and other issues that were a daily part of single parenting. How could I ever express what was lost between a husband and a wife? How could I voice to others what was only ours to share?

At times I was engulfed by the vacuum that existed in daily life. No more phone calls or text messages from my husband. No more sharing the bathroom mirror or cuddling in bed. No one to call for directions or to consult on financial decisions. No one to grow old beside me.

My abandonment was a humiliation. It was as if my husband had said to others, "I've used this long enough. If anyone else wants it, just take it."

I had been discarded and placed at the curb like any other pile of rubbish, and my shame was visible to all. It was difficult to venture into public places, to carry out even the most routine chores.

One day I was shopping with my daughters. They had each selected a pair of shoes from the sale rack, and we headed to the checkout counter. In that moment I was gripped by a sudden and unreasonable fear. As I handed over my debit card to complete the transaction, a suffocating sense of panic hijacked my logic. "What if that's her behind the counter? She sees my name, she knows who I am, and she's mocking me."

What should have been a friendly interchange with a sales clerk became a threat. This panic-like experience was repeated again and again at the grocery store, the school auditorium, the gas station, and every other public place. My shame hovered like a dark cloud, and I felt it so intensely that I assumed it was seen by everyone I encountered.

I had never been plagued by clinical depression, but grief did drag me through at least some symptoms of depression. It was difficult to face life, and I had a tendency to withdraw by avoiding people, refusing to answer calls, and sleeping for extended periods of time. I was physically and emotionally drained by rejection, and the why was still unanswered. The majority of my waking moments were consumed by self-doubt and heartache. Even in sleep my fears and hurts found expression in troubling dreams.

There were times when I didn't have the courage to keep going during this protracted period of grief. I wanted so badly to stop the pain, and sometimes I considered measures that were far outside the norm of my thinking. I was tempted to drink my pain away. I thought about how I might find acceptance in the arms of another man. I even toyed with the idea of an overdose to kill all feeling.

Each of these ideas held some promise of relief. Fortunately, I had enough sense to recognize them as alternate paths in the darkness of the tunnel; when I didn't have enough sense, I had faithful friends to redirect me.

Three months after my final split from Rick, I went to a high-school football game where my daughter's dance team was going to perform at halftime. A number of friends and family members joined me. Rick was also at the game, and he brought his girlfriend. Everyone around me knew she was there, and it felt as if my shame had somehow been projected for all to see. Distress is too understated a word to describe how I felt by the time I returned home. I paced back and forth on the sidewalk, refusing to go into the house. I couldn't face the pain, and I didn't trust myself. I knew the remainder of a prescription painkiller was sitting untouched in my medicine cabinet. Swallowing a handful of pills and ending my life would have been an easy choice.

Finally I called a faithful friend and shared my fears. It was hard to be so transparent and to admit such desperation, but I needed her. I truly felt that I could not live one more moment with the pain, and I told her so. I knew what she would say to me about burying my pain with drugs. I knew she would tell me about living for my children and my future. I knew what she would say, and that's why I called her. I did not want to hurt myself, but in that moment I didn't want to live either. I needed someone there with me in that oppressing crevice of the tunnel, a voice of comfort, someone who could see the exit that remained invisible to me.

At this point, the tunnel was endless. I wandered aimlessly without hope. I existed, but I did not live. Thankfully I was not totally alone. God was there to guide me. In truth, he had been beside me since I first entered the tunnel, and he had watched over me as I had taken each halting step. When I reached those points that were more than I could bear, he drew near to nudge me forward.

He accepted and honored my infinitesimal speck of faith. I didn't need to move mountains like the one who possesses the proverbial mustard seed. I just needed to survive for one day and then another. Surely I had courage enough for that.

I could continue to walk a little farther, knowing that he was walking with me in the darkness, believing that, somehow, he would guide me to the light that did exist on the other side.

Dear Liv,

You are such an amazing friend. I don't know how you do it, honestly. No matter how much I call on you, you are there. You have your own troubles, and I know some of them are very heavy for you right now, but when we're together, you put my needs ahead of your own.

You never minimize the loss I am feeling. You let me grieve. I don't think I have ever possessed such compassion for others, but thank God you do. I hope, when this is all over, I can be half as good a friend to others as you have been to me.

Thank you, Liv, for hurrying to my side the other night (again). I was so afraid, and I knew I needed to call someone. I have never thought about doing anything like that before. I don't know what might have happened if you hadn't come or if you hadn't helped me remember how much I had to live for.

Thank you for staying beside me until those feelings of panic and desperation went away. Thank you for constantly fighting for me when I am too weak to fight for myself. And thank you for not judging me or lecturing me. I knew my reasoning was all wrong, but at that moment, I couldn't help it.

No matter what life brings, I am fortunate to have a friend like you.

Always grateful,
Your friend in need

Dirty Scoundrel

When they hurled their insults at him,
he did not retaliate;
when he suffered, he made no threats.
Instead, he entrusted himself to
him who judges justly.
I Peter 2:23

By this time my hold on the past was tenuous. I could never regain my life by backtracking to the place where I had entered the tunnel of grief. On the other hand, the path before me remained unknown.

I had no guarantee that I would ever escape the pain and loneliness that enveloped me. I was trapped, and I was alone. I began to feel the injustice of my circumstance. Him! This was all his fault. He had pushed me into this place and left me alone in the dark. He knew there was no way out, but he didn't care enough to make sure I would survive. How could he? How could he!

I began to recount the reasons I deserved better. For eighteen years I had been a faithful wife. I had managed the household, paid the bills, filed the taxes, and handled household repairs. I had gone without vacations, luxuries, and trinkets that other women might have considered necessary tokens of love. I had forgiven the purchase of innumerable cars, trucks, and motorcycles, each bought on a whim without my consultation and to my financial detriment. I had watched my savings dwindle, never to be replaced. I had overlooked circumstances that pointed to infidelity, accepting feeble and illogical excuses. I had remained committed despite broken promises, because I believed that somehow our future was worth the trouble.

This is what I deserved? He stole my future, my intimacy, my security, and my pride. He left me with nothing. Why should his life go on uninterrupted, after he had so totally destroyed mine?

I raced frantically back and forth in this stretch of the tunnel, screaming for a solution, demanding a way out. I pounded furiously on the walls, scratching away at the ceiling, and even trying to claw my way through the ground beneath me. I wanted the maddening torment to stop. Resentment began to singe the flesh of my heart, and every reminder fed the flame of hatred that was growing within me.

A flame can be controlled, for a while. Continually fed, it becomes a raging fire of destruction. Anger is the same. It destroys the heart of flesh, burning a deep black hole. At the very bottom of that gaping hole, bitterness takes root. My bitterness began to advance rapidly, and I did not recognize how much of my heart and mind had been overtaken. It sucked the nutrients from the once-fertile soil of my life and left me parched, unfruitful, unpleasant—and still alone.

Though Rick had inflicted my pain, I knew that the only choice I had was to manage the resulting anger and bitterness. Thankfully, in his time, God pointed a fatherly finger toward my renegade thoughts. He shined a light on the troublesome root that was taking hold within me, and he offered a solution.

Ironically, the very day Rick chose to walk away from our marriage, I received the results of a biopsy that revealed abnormal cell growth. The doctor recommended surgery to remove the abnormal cells that were encapsulated within otherwise healthy tissue. This procedure, he explained, would prevent the troublesome cells from invading the healthy tissue. Ignoring the abnormality could be dangerous, but the choice was mine. Twenty-one days after Rick walked away, my son drove me to the hospital for surgery.

I knew that allowing God to remove my root of bitterness would be a similar process. It too was an elective procedure. God had the power to excise the root, but I had to be agreeable to the plan of treatment. I had to trust this spiritual physician to do what was best for me, to remove the bitterness that would otherwise overtake what remained of my life.

I had experienced anger toward Rick during our four-month attempt at reconciliation, but it was not my most evident response. Our marriage counselor one day challenged me, "So where is your anger in all this?"

"Oh, it's here," I assured him, and I took a moment to recount a few outbursts of anger. There was the time I found a woman's shirt in the midst of Rick's laundry after he had moved back home. Faced with the tangible reminder of the other woman, I momentarily lost my cool. There was the time I kicked and splintered the wicker planter in my living room. Yes, I had experienced anger over the adultery and the deceit and the rejection.

After our marriage had totally dissolved, I had other bouts of anger, times when I said things to Rick or about him that reflected the blame I knew he deserved. Nothing, however, compared to the overwhelming anger that settled in my heart and mind one full year after he was gone for good.

It was August again, and so much had happened in the span of that one year. I had moved across the country, I was three months into a new career, and I was ready to move into a new home, my home. After a full year of uncertainty and the need to rely financially on others, my life was finally getting back on track.

I received the keys to my newly purchased house on Friday, and on Saturday morning I was loading my car to make my final move. It would take only a few trips from my brother's home to mine, because I had left most of my belongings behind when I had moved one year before. It was 10:00 a.m. when I received a phone call that plunged me into a fit of anger greater than any I had experienced to that point. I received news of the birth of a baby, born to Rick and his girlfriend, born on the very day I was taking possession of my new home.

Could I not have one day that was mine, one day that was not marred by him and his selfish choices?

In that moment I was pulled back to the very center of that long tunnel, enveloped by darkness, void of hope. I thought I had left the worst of the ugliness and pain behind me, but I could not free myself of this new round of crushing anger. I knew that my husband had left me for another woman. I knew there was a baby on the way. I knew the facts, but nothing could have prepared me for such a devastating relapse.

Emotionally, I was thrown back to the beginning of my journey. I had the same feelings of panic in busy, public places. I had the same desire to withdraw into a shell, to hide myself and my shame from the world. My anger was so deep and so thick that it oozed out with every word and thought and behavior.

One afternoon I was able to hear my anger spilling out onto my daughters, and I saw the frustration on their faces. Their pained expressions triggered an alarm inside of me, calling me from the depths of my own self-pity. As a mother I knew it was time to prioritize the needs of my children. They had enough emotional upheaval to manage without carrying my burdens. It was time to battle the bitterness that had begun to rule my life.

While Rick had laid the cornerstones of pain, I was responsible for what was constructed on top of that foundation. My contribution began with the careful stacking of one brick after another, each one a reminder of a hurt inflicted upon me. Though I didn't realize it at the time, I was constructing walls of anger, jealousy, resentment, and self-pity.

As I looked into the faces of my girls, I realized I could not be an effective parent until I dismantled the walls that imprisoned me, and I knew of only one way to do that.

Forgiveness.

I struggled with the idea. It seemed unfair to grant forgiveness to someone who was so undeserving. On the other hand, I knew forgiveness was the key to my release. I needed freedom from the suffocating torment of bitterness, freedom to heal, and freedom to explore all that life still had to offer. It was time for the walls to come down. In that moment I made the conscious decision to free myself from the prison of bitterness.

Forgiveness, I learned, is a process. It is a choice made in a moment, again and again and again. The anger of my circumstance resurfaced, sometimes so unexpectedly and with such ferocity that I questioned my ability to ever fully forgive. Each day it became important only that I decided to forgive, not that my success was lasting. I cycled in and out of the process of forgiveness. I tried and I failed, but God honored my choice to obey.

At this point in my journey, I was still very deep inside the darkness of the tunnel. I saw no evidence of light. Though I was moving, I couldn't be certain that it was forward. It was more like being shoved along by the power of a strong current. The direction was not of my choosing, and I had no clue where I was headed. I did, however, have the choice to forgive.

Dear Liv,

I never thought of myself as a hateful person, but maybe I am. All I do is tell the same stories and voice the same anger, over and over. Only a true friend like you would stick by me through this mess—and keep listening!

So much hurt, such a feeling of being abandoned. I think it all comes to the surface in ugly words and lousy attitudes. In my heart, I know I'll eventually move past this anger, but I sure am losing the battle right now. Thanks, Liv, for accepting me just the way I am.

By the way, I just got some great advice—again. You know, the "If he's going to be like that, you'll be better off without him" kind of thing. I guess people mean well, but when they give me their sweet little smiles and their trite lines of wisdom, I want to scream. "Maybe I don't think I'll be better off. Maybe I don't want to be alone!" Seriously, some people must think that getting through a divorce is like getting over the flu.

You're one of the few people who really understands the way I feel right now. I still want my husband, not a replacement. I want my family together again. I want my life back.

Today I feel like I can't see one step in front of me. Everything is dark. Ahead of me, behind me—I see nothing but darkness. I'll keep fighting though, Liv, because I know better than to let you down!

Be patient—I'm working on it.

Not forever,
Your angry friend

Green-Eyed Monster

You know how I am scorned,
disgraced and shamed;
all my enemies are before you.
Scorn has broken my heart and
has left me helpless.
Psalm 69:19–20a

I was living in Texas in September 2008 when ominous cloud coverage swirled above the Gulf Coast, signaling impending doom. Hurricane Ike rolled in, pummeling the coast, flooding historic Galveston landmarks and homes with no regard for tradition or personal attachment. Entire foundations were swept away. Ike's four-day tryst caused far-reaching devastation, and the process of recovery was extensive as victims struggled to rebuild.

I likened Rick's infidelity to this catastrophe of nature. Two people met, and they decided that their selfish desires were more important than anything else. Their choices set in motion a destructive chain of events. Integrity was crushed. Betrayal demolished the tradition and sanctity of marriage. The foundation of our family was swept away, and my children and I were left unprotected, directly in the storm's path, with no choice but to absorb its fury.

How can I convey the agony of infidelity? It was knowledge I did not want to have. It was an uncovering of what I held most private, the relinquishment of what was mine alone. It was nakedness and shame. It was rejection in its most blatant form as my spouse said to me, "I know you better than anyone else knows you, and I want more than you can offer." It was an act that swiftly and completely crushed my self-worth. Why would the one who vowed to forever love and protect me now choose so freely to abandon me?

It was impossible to envision a resident of Galveston Island murmuring a few parting words and then abandoning his family as Hurricane Ike prepared to hit land. "I'm going to leave now. I have removed the hurricane shutters and protective plywood from the windows. I know you have no batteries, cash, or drinking water, but you'll be fine. I have to go now. Someone else needs my protection from the storm."

Someone else. It was so difficult to voice, and even more challenging to accept. The betrayal carved dead-end paths into an already hazardous maze of grief. Each path was littered with haunting voices and disturbing images. Though I sought escape, I was destined to encounter reminders of the betrayal again and again. I considered each routine I had once shared with my husband: nicknames, holiday traditions, silly songs, nighttime rituals. I wondered if he had revealed these confidences to her as well.

I cringed as I realized how many lies had passed between us. Nothing was sacred, and I was bombarded with one realization after another. Over time I began to see more clearly. I recognized as obvious lies the circumstances I had once accepted blindly. The veil of trust had been removed, and the truth became painfully clear.

As a police officer, Rick had always found time to stop by our house on Christmas morning when the kids opened presents, even if it was a bit removed from his regular beat. It was very painful when, in hindsight, I realized why he had not come home to be with us on the morning of our final Christmas as a married couple. He had chosen to spend Christmas morning away from home, watching someone else open gifts.

I understood why he could never get a vacation schedule that coincided with mine, yet he found ways to take days off when I was working. I understood why he used a password to guard his phone and why he worked so many extra hours providing overnight security at an area hotel. I understood, and I wished I did not.

Every undetected phone call, every clandestine meeting, every penny spent, every forbidden touch—it was all territory plundered from the secure boundaries of our marriage.

The definition of jealousy is to be possessively watchful, demanding exclusive loyalty. It is to feel suspicious about a competitor's influence, especially in regard to a loved one. I was possessive of my spouse, and I expected loyalty. I was suspicious and bitter toward anyone who interfered with this loyalty. It is logical that I felt nothing less than jealousy when confronted with my spouse's infidelity and the knowledge that he favored another over me.

Unchecked jealousy, however, can become a dangerous dictator. It can capture the mind and incite a hunger for revenge. While jealousy is a natural emotion, revenge is a forbidden behavior. My anger was justified, but I could not afford to waste my limited emotional resources on spiteful phone calls, desperate tracking measures or any other means of retribution.

I could not yet understand how or when God would restore me, but I had to walk forward believing that he would.

Dear Liv,

I know you say the shame belongs to Rick, but in my heart and mind it is my shame. I cannot voice the torment or convey the haunting images that I face each day. Every place I go, I wonder if they have been there together. Does this waitress know? Have they sat in these movie seats together? Did they meet at that hotel?

When I roll over in bed at night and my arm rests on his empty place, I weep. I know where he is, and I know what he's doing. I am nothing more than worthless, discarded trash. I cannot comprehend all the things that must be wrong with me, that would cause him to utterly reject me. I cannot bear the humiliation of their conversations and laughter, the ridicule they have shared at my expense.

I trusted, loved, worked, and managed my home. I was a faithful wife. He lied, cheated, and abandoned his responsibilities.

He is a faithless man. It is not just that I am alone. I am alone with the thoughts, the reminders, and the heartache.

Why do people insist on asking me her name or what she looks like? The unknown is torment, but the known is pain I cannot bear. When someone speaks her name, she becomes a real person. Against my will I am engaged in a one-to-one competition, and I am the loser. I want people to quit telling me what they have heard about her or what they think of her. Don't they get it? I don't want to talk about her. She lives in my mind already as a haunting vision, and her very existence is a continuous stabbing motion to my heart.

One thing I do know. I will never give her—them—the power of knowing the pain they have caused me. I will hold my head up, knowing that I am cut from a different fabric. I will never stoop to trading ugly phone calls. I will never show up on her doorstep to make empty claims. I will never give herthe time of day or allow her to make me less than I am.

I don't think there is much I can do right now but live one day at a time. I suppose the pain will one day subside, though I can't imagine it right now. God help me, that's all I can say.

Stick with me, good friend. I don't think I can make it without you.

Once again,
Your feeling-sorry-for-herself friend

Chin Up, Chin Down

I know what it is to be in need,
and I know what it is to have plenty.
Philippians 4:12a

I noticed a flicker of light and sensed that I was beginning the final stretch of my journey. In certain areas the heavy darkness remained unchallenged. For the first time, however, I sensed that hope did exist beyond the foreboding walls of the tunnel. It was something I could not reach, something that still could not reach me. But it was out there, I knew.

Each day would bring one more trace of light, a quick flash, a lingering ray. Over time I noticed that beams of light had begun to fully penetrate the walls that surrounded me, at least in places. Eventually the light illuminated the path before me, and I could logically evaluate my journey, perhaps for the first time.

I faced a figurative three-way mirror, and each reflection suggested an alternate outcome. As I looked to the left, I saw an intelligent, professional, and capable woman. She was charting her own course in life, forging new relationships, establishing a new career, and reclaiming her confidence. I admired her courage and strength.

The reflection to the right was vastly different. Here I looked into the face of discouragement and glimpsed a posture of hopelessness and defeat. This woman seemed an empty shell, void of physical and emotional appeal. I feared that her future held no promise.

The middle reflection revealed a combination of strength and weakness, contentment and despair. It was an obvious blend of the first two images. I could tell this woman had potential, but I wasn't certain she had the stamina to overcome the wounds of her past or the courage to create a new future for herself. I knew this image was most realistic, a true reflection of my own life.

It was a confusing time. It was also a time of awakening, a time when I recognized that I had the power to choose my own outcome. I could choose to remain the victim of my circumstance and crawl through life, hampered by the burden of someone else's choices. My other option was to lay aside the weight of the past and walk with purpose toward the exit of the tunnel.

I have seen news reports that tell the story of miners trapped far below the earth's surface. Hours of waiting can turn to days of despair, but once the promise of rescue is given, hope rushes in to penetrate the darkness. Parched and tired men are renewed, and their spirits are lifted even before the rescue is accomplished.

In some small way I recognized that my celebration could also begin before the suffering ended. I began to grasp the realization that my pain would one day cease. I knew that the tunnel's exit was ahead, and I no longer feared that darkness would swallow what remained of my life.

Freedom did not come in an instant, however. The exit was in my line of vision, but the pathway was not yet clear. It would take time and effort to complete my journey of grief.

I experienced a cyclical pattern of hope and despair. One day I was ready to move forward with my life, daring to be excited about new possibilities. Boldly I would share with friends that my grief had lifted. Then the sun would set, not only at the end of my literal day, but also on my newly proclaimed hope. A familiar heaviness would settle, and I would begrudge its return.

Why did I have to be burdened again with darkness? In theory, I was already free from the past. In practicality, I had a long way to go before my new life was established. Minor circumstances sometimes brought this painfully to light.

One beautiful day, when my daughters and I still lived in my brother's home, I was particularly full of optimism. Everyone had plans and quickly scattered in their own directions. Once I was alone in the house, I was pulled from the height of optimism down into the pit of despair. The plunge was instant. Hours later, when everyone had returned from their activities, I was still sobbing. I was grieving my lack of connection, mourning the loss of relationships that had been or that should have been. I regretted the fact that I had lived far from my roots for most of my adult life, and now I had returned with little to show for my years away. In that moment, the process of rebuilding seemed impossible.

To taste emotional freedom and then have it pulled from my grasp was frustrating. I knew that I needed to stand firm and wait for the crush of circumstance to pass. The battle wouldn't rage forever, but I had to accept that I still dwelled in the tunnel.

Discouraging words lingered in the crevices, and taunting images lurked around corners. There were low spots of shame and hopelessness yet to be crossed and places of uncertainty that awaited me.

Thankfully, the path ahead was not nearly as treacherous as what I had left behind. My job was to keep walking over and around the remaining obstacles. To give up now would be foolishness.

For the remainder of my journey, contentment and sorrow coexisted. Morning would bring a wave of optimism and the scent of new life. The birds would serenade me, and the sun would shine just to give me warmth. By nightfall I would mourn and weep, convinced that I was a rejected and worthless being.

This process repeated itself many times as I fought to regain my emotional equilibrium. I was in transition, moving out of darkness and into the fresh, untrampled path of a new life.

One day I would look back at a tunnel that had been sealed, never to be traveled again. Its dark, oppressive passages would be only a memory. It was for this hope that I kept walking.

Dear Liv,

It's been a while, hasn't it? Things are finally beginning to shift a little, but not quite fast enough. If I could have seen one year ago how long it would take to get where I am today, I don't know if I would have even tried. I never imagined that anything could hurt so badly for this long.

There are still days when I feel as if the darkness will never depart. I might wake up on top of the world, and then by evening I am grieving all over again. I'm excited about my future, and then I mourn the fact that I am alone. My emotions swing from one extreme to the other. The good news is that the lows don't come as often, and they don't last as long. I am happy more often. I'll bet you're glad to finally hear that!

I miss being close enough to get coffee with you, and I miss all the wisdom you shared with me. I'm sure you won't be surprised when I say that you were right about many things. Just like you told me, life is getting better. I'm not positive, but I think there is more light than darkness now. I get the feeling that the light has always been there, but for some reason I can finally see it.

One of these days, Liv, I will tell people about a tiny beam of light that was powerful enough to pierce the darkness in my life. I'll tell them how the tiny beam brought hope, and how the light helped turn despair to praise and transform brokenness to beauty.

You, my friend, have been that tiny beam of light.

Thank you for helping to pierce the darkness, Your grateful friend

The Proceedings

For this reason a man will leave
his father and mother
and be united to his wife, and the two
will become one flesh.
So they are no longer two, but one.
Therefore what God has joined together,
let man not separate.
Matthew 19:5–6

I remember when I finally neared the elusive exit to the tunnel. This, I thought, would be my final step out of grief.

I squinted my eyes as I stood at the threshold of a new life. I was so accustomed to the darkness of my long journey that I was hesitant to move forward, even though I was tempted by the bright and open path that lay ahead. It is not that I found any security or comfort in the tunnel or any reason that I should want to spend more time there. It did represent, however, all that I had known for a very long time.

Now here I was on the threshold, ready to be thrust once again onto a new path. It was brighter, that much I knew, but it was also unknown. I was preparing to leave behind all that was familiar. That piece of my past would soon be sealed, and I would never again revisit the relationship that had once been my very life.

The final and tangible acts of divorce, such as mediation, facing a judge, and signing the decree, reignited the emotions of my journey. As I prepared for what I thought would be the final step, the one that would forever expel me from the tunnel of grief, I was assailed by a jumble of pain, shame, despair, and resentment. I had battled these foes for a very long time. The divorce, I had hoped, would bring a definite end to my long journey. Instead, I was confronted with the permanence of my loss.

When a loved one suffers with a terminal illness, people often say that death is preferred. Yet when we close the coffin lid, we experience pain, not joy. For me, finalizing the divorce was similar. My marriage had been destroyed, and I no longer held any illusion of survival. To close the lid, however, by finalizing the divorce was a very difficult step. It was an acknowledgment that hope had ceased, and it sealed an unhappy ending to a significant chapter of my life.

The divorce court itself was a surreal environment. The door seemed to revolve incessantly, a gateway through which the disgruntled and the heartbroken passed. In hallways outside the courtroom, lawyers were striking last-minute deals with anxious spouses. Inside, the bailiff was sitting quietly, occasionally making obligatory rounds of the courtroom to chastise those using a cell phone or reading anything other than a court document. After each round, he would sit again. Lawyers lugged imposing files to the front to check docket times with the court clerk. Men and women claimed a spot on the hard courtroom benches, nervously awaiting the call of their names. They listened half-heartedly to the droning voices that drifted down from the bench before them.

"Raise your right hand, and repeat after me," the judge politely instructed. "Do you swear to tell the whole truth in the testimony you are about to give?"

The respondent's faint "I do" carried the proceedings forward.

A series of basic inquiries followed: "State your full name. Were you married to John Doe on or about July 18, 1993? Do you agree that your marriage is insupportable because of conflict between the two of you? Is there any chance this marriage can be reconciled?"

Barely audible responses were intermittently offered: "Jane Doe...Yes...Yes...No."

"Based on your testimony," the judge pronounced, "your decree is granted by the court."

Your decree is granted. The choice of words made the process sound quite pleasant. My decree had been granted, as if a genie had just bestowed upon me the dream of a lifetime.

I had just signed the death certificate for my eighteen-year marriage before a crowd of unknown spectators. I had been separated forever from the one who had promised to be joined to me for a lifetime. My dreams of a happy marriage and a bright future had disintegrated, and my children would be forever impacted. No dreams had been granted that day.

As I exited the courtroom alone, I realized that my emotional turmoil would not be quieted. The judge had legally sanctioned the end of my marital status, but it was not the ending I had sought. It was another beginning. Fortunately, it was the beginning of the final leg of my journey.

Rather than succumb to discouragement, I used this time to look back and appreciate my progress. While the divorce proceedings did represent an emotional setback, I had not surrendered already-conquered territory. I had survived shock. I had learned to manage my anger, and I was beginning to shrug off the oppressive guilt. I truly did stand at the threshold of a new life.

I knew I would have to be alert, careful to avoid tempting paths that would dead-end in renewed bitterness or revenge. If I did find myself slipping into that destructive mode, I would need to redirect my energy and choose a path that would continue to lead me away from the tunnel. A bright future awaited me, but I had to walk toward it with purpose and courage.

With each step, the oppressive yoke of pain and shame was sliding from my shoulders. I knew I would one day walk unhindered, free from the hurt that had kept me bound for so long. How sad it would be if I refused this freedom and instead choose to labor under the weight of the past.

Dear Liv,

It was tough being back in town to finish up all the "details." It was good to see you, though. Thanks for taking time for lunch. I think you were the only one who didn't ask me if I got everything I wanted.

Each time I heard that question, I wanted to lash out, "Oh yes! Everything I wanted. I wanted to have a broken family, no home, and no future. I wanted to be rejected, replaced, and alone!" They meant well (I guess), so I didn't say anything. But really, did they think I came back to make sure I got the dining room table and the couch?

I don't blame anyone. I actually thought I would be ready to celebrate. I had planned to erase each e-mail, text, and voice mail from him today, a ceremonial cleansing of sorts. I was surprised that I wasn't ready to do it. I know it's over, but I guess I have to grieve awhile longer. Today hurt a lot more than I expected.

As I head back to my new home and my new life, I know that one of the things I'll miss most is being able to call on you, day and night. What a faithful friend you have been, but I guess it's time for me to move along and live like a big girl!

To friendship that reaches beyond the miles!
Your ready-to-move-on friend

A New Song

I waited patiently for the LORD;
he turned to me and heard my cry.
He lifted me out of the slimy pit,
out of the mud and mire;
He set my feet on a rock and
gave me a firm place to stand.
He put a new song in my mouth,
a hymn of praise to our God.
Many will see and fear
and put their trust in the LORD.

Psalm 40:1–3

There was no definitive moment when the future became more important than the past. One day I simply realized that the momentum of life had shifted. The torment had subsided, and I was no longer consumed with yesterday.

There were definitely setbacks, times when a dull ache persisted even as life moved along. An elderly couple walking hand in hand would remind me that my partner chose not to stand by through thick and thin, for better or worse. A couple engaged in quiet conversation over dinner made me long for companionship.

During those moments I felt a sense of loss. Those twinges, however, paled in comparison to the overwhelming pain that once rocked my world each and every day. They no longer had the power to fling me back into the emotional abyss.

Scars were beginning to appear where wounds once festered. I naturally felt some discomfort as those still tender areas were pulled and stretched by the growth of a new life. I understood that it was all part of the healing process.

I realized that I was standing, for the first time in more than a year, outside of the tunnel. I looked toward the past with a mixture of relief and amazement. I had survived my journey of grief! For a time, it was enough simply to enjoy that knowledge. I had no desire to jump back into the many roles that I had once filled in life.

I stood still and surveyed the view, occasionally looking back over my shoulder to revel in the fact that the tunnel exit was indeed sealed. I would never again retrace those steps. Freshness had replaced the stagnant oppressiveness of grief, and it felt good to breathe in the faint scent of hope. The refreshing breeze that washed over me carried a sense of expectation, but I was very content to remain still and simply enjoy these new sensations.

During this time I made tremendous strides in life. I delved into the learning curve of a new career, the parenting of teenage daughters, and the establishment of a new home. I was one step past survival, but I did not yet have the strength to venture beyond the basic requirements of daily living. I spent close to two years in this mode, gaining strength, overcoming minor setbacks, and taking baby steps forward.

Eventually the scenery around me began to change, or perhaps my perception of that scenery changed. In every direction I was beckoned by the vibrant images of life. I saw, as if for the first time, the pudgy face of an adorable toddler, the calm magnificence of a starry night, the fragile beauty of a butterfly. I heard the wisdom of an old man, the sounds of children playing and the conversation of good friends. I was drawn by these sights and sounds, and I felt a longing to rejoin the circles of life that had for so long been outside my reach. I was prepared to consciously walk forward into my new life, though I had no idea which path I should follow. What I did know, however, was that the decision was mine.

A few particular experiences began to define my reentry into life. In and of themselves, they were insignificant. To me, however, they served to reinforce the knowledge that I was healing. Life began to take on meaning, and that meaning was no longer a reflection of my past. Each new experience snapped a symbolic cord of bondage, and with the breaking of each cord, a somehow audible "ping" of recognition resonated within me. My heart and mind were opening to absorb the hope of a restored life, and I knew that I would once again find purpose in life and in relationship.

Young people had always been an important part of my life. I had spent years pouring into the lives of teens and young adults. It had been my passion and a defining part of who I was. With the upheaval of my divorce and a cross-country move, I had lost those connections, and in some ways I had lost the vision that I could ever again be that person.

For that reason Derek was a bright spot, a momentary interaction that awakened something within me, stirring a vision of what my future might still hold.

Derek was probably about ten years old when I met him in the bumper-car queue at a dated amusement park in the central part of the state. I already had my eye on bumper car number six, and he was headed for number three. I sent him a quick signal, requesting that he help me gang up on my friend who was slipping into car number one. At that point, I didn't know Derek's name and we had not spoken a single word, but that didn't matter. Bumper cars have a way of speeding relationship building. Derek and I formed a partnership with that brief signal.

When the cars began to move, we raced after car number one. For the next few moments our cars circled the track, and we shared the fun and freedom of ramming others. When the cars came to a stop, I looked toward my young friend and gave him a thumbs-up to thank him for his help. He took a few steps, and then he stopped. He turned back toward me with his hand outstretched and said, "Hi, I'm Derek."

I was moved by this uncommonly mature gesture from such a young boy. We exchanged a few more friendly words before he went his own way.

That brief interchange reminded me of the work I had done and the lives of the children I had touched. I also glimpsed a vision of the opportunities that might still lie ahead. In that moment I knew those same God-given passions remained a part of me.

Ping! I felt, or heard, the restrictive cord of self-doubt give way. Circumstance may have dampened the intensity and interrupted the delivery of my passion, but I knew then that the source was still intact.

I was content with the little house I had purchased. It was all I needed, and it was mine. In those first few years of singleness, it was enough to know that I owned a home, and I was absorbed by the responsibilities of managing it. There came a day, however, when I knew I was ready to make that little house my own. I was ready to transition from survival to settled, from a roof over my head to a home that I loved. I began to explore paint colors, new flooring, and kitchen designs.

Ping! Another cord snapped as I moved from acceptance of my circumstance to anticipation of my future.

I was introduced to Tim through a mutual friend. Days later he called, and I made my way nervously through the conversation. He called again, and the words flowed more easily. The hundreds of miles between us created a comfortable barrier, and I began to look forward to the calls that came almost daily. Eventually I was able to grasp the reality of a relationship, a friendship that understood the heartaches of divorce and the challenges of single parenting. It was emotionally rewarding to share, to give love, and to receive love.

Ping! Another cord snapped as I, against all odds, ventured to build a relationship of trust.

"When the valley is deep and the mountain is steep," the choir sang out, "when your resources are spent and you're battled and scarred, press on."

Surely I had heard the song before, but on this particular Sunday morning, more than two years beyond the breakup of my marriage, it struck a new chord. For so long I had been laboring under the heaviness that my faith in God had been destroyed. I did not feel that God cared for me, and I wondered how much true faith remained in my heart. Somehow the reminder to press on brought clarity to my heart, mind, and soul that morning. I did believe.

Ping! What heaviness lifted when I realized that God had been holding me all along, and that he was still holding me. I had passed through the tunnel, and he was beginning to usher me out of the haze that had for so long clouded my self-perceptions and my ability to recognize his love for me.

As one cord after another snapped, my view of the future expanded. Instead of trudging through grief or battling the strenuous uphill journey of despair, I felt as if I was running downhill, traveling so fast that I could barely control my eagerness and desire to explore the new and exciting paths before me. Something in me had been awakened, and I was ready to enjoy whatever the rest of life might bring.

I raced forward with abandon.

Dear Liv,

There is so much going on in my life! Who would have thought I would ever get to this point? Remember when I used to complain about Rick, "I know where he is, and I know what he's doing?" That always hurt me so much. Now when I speak those same words, I smile. Yes, I do know where he is and what he's doing, and it doesn't matter anymore. I can think about my life now, not what he took from me. In so many ways, I'm thankful to be free.

I could not have reached this point without you. You have been with me since day one. You stood by me in my anger. You supported me when I was so depressed. You listened to me for hours on end, always patient, always loving. I will never be able to thank you enough. God put you in my life for a very special purpose.

As you watch me walk forward in this new life, know that you are one reason I can sing a new song!

With love,
Your forever grateful friend

Epilogue

In the Driver's Seat

*I instruct you in the way of wisdom
and lead you along straight paths.*
Proverbs 4:11

I chased a lot of dreams as I raced down that hill of newfound freedom. It was an alternately exhilarating and frustrating journey. I would spy an opportunity and run full speed in pursuit, certain the answers I sought could be found in that one experience. Then my attention would be drawn in another direction, and off I would go, convinced that this new path would offer all that I was seeking. Before long that chase would end as well, and I would again stand frustrated and empty-handed. After a handful of false starts, I began to grow disenchanted.

The untested paths before me seemed limitless, but I had no guarantee that any would lead to a destination of my choosing. I was challenged by the need to make every decision on my own.

On my own. That realization became a burden. I lost sight of the adventure I had begun, and I became focused instead on the fact that I had no one to accompany me on my journey. My enthusiasm waned, and my pace began to slow. I longed to hitch a ride with someone who was passing by, jump into the passenger seat, and relax. With someone else behind the wheel, the decisions wouldn't all have to be mine.

I found a fairly comfortable place by the side of the road, and I waited. I watched as multitudes passed by, heading with purpose to one destination or another. Still I sat. My frustration grew. How could so many pass me by, totally unconcerned that I was waiting for a ride? Was there no man who would open his door, invite me to accompany him, and carry me forward? I continued to wait, rather impatiently. How quickly I had forgotten the oppressiveness of the tunnel and the freedom I had so recently celebrated.

Finally, someone ventured near. He pulled slightly to the side of the road where I sat, rolled down his window and chatted a bit. I thought he might open the passenger door and invite me to join him. He didn't. Instead he pulled forward and prepared to merge with the other moving traffic. Before he had ventured too far, I stopped him. I wanted to understand why he had chosen to drive away so suddenly.

His words of explanation stung a bit: *What you need to do is get in the driver's seat.*

There was no judgment or harshness in his tone, just the straightforward approach of one friend advising another. Such a simple phrase. Such a powerful thought.

What you need to do is get in the driver's seat. Decide where you want to take your life, and then maybe someday someone will come along who is going in the same direction as you.

I turned his words over in my mind. I was intrigued by the potential of what my life might become if I truly climbed into the driver's seat and steered my life in the direction of my own choosing.

I thought I had learned all I needed to know during my trek through the tunnel. I realized, however, that though my grief had ended, my journey was still in process. That simple phrase became a measuring stick, a means of evaluating each of my expectations and behaviors along the way.

What you need to do is get in the driver's seat. His unspoken message became clearer as I considered it objectively. *No one, including me, is going to arrive on the scene with a ready-made life designed just for you. I am not here to save you from your past, and I am not here to create your future. That's for you to do.*

His words only stung because they were true. I had slipped into the subconscious expectation that someone would come along and give me the life I wanted. I had been looking for that one relationship that would complete me, make my life easier, and provide a clear path that I could follow. I understood then that I needed to shift my expectations. I had been seeking a void-filler. The risk was that I might end up pounding an unfit peg into the empty spot in my heart. The true challenge before me was to establish a new life, my new life.

I thanked him for his advice and watched him pull away. It was time for me to call on a new kind of strength. It was time for me to get into the driver's seat and steer my life in the direction of my choosing.

Suddenly I realized that the downhill slope had ended. I now surveyed a broad expanse of level land, an image of life stretching before me as far as I could see in every direction. Once again the opportunities called to me, but this time I heard a chorus of sweet invitations to enjoy my journey regardless of the destination.

I began by accepting my need to establish life as a single woman. For so long, my focus had revolved around husband, children, and the obligations of family life. Bringing my thoughts into alignment with a completely new lifestyle required consistent effort and mental training. Eventually I was able to envision what my new life could become.

I also evaluated my view of men and the possibility of future relationships. My expectations shifted in unison with the increasing value I placed on my own worth as a woman. A simple thought surfaced, and I recognized and accepted it as a healthy guideline: *A kiss is not just a kiss. It is a tiny piece of my heart offered up in the hope of receiving affection and affirmation. When that kiss is no longer shared, that tiny fragment of my heart will suffer.*

My habit had always been to give my trust freely, withdrawing it only after it had been continuously disregarded and eventually decimated. I knew, going forward, that I would need to find a balance, demanding evidence of trustworthiness without creating a barrier that would make a relationship impossible. That careful balance would no doubt take practice, but I was convinced that the right man would have the patience and desire to earn my trust, my respect, and my affection.

I had turned yet another corner in my journey, and the transition was positive. Planning my trip became a joy rather than a burden. I forged new friendships and embraced every new opportunity that came my way. Life was invigorating, and I was no longer afraid to go it alone. I became more and more comfortable in the driver's seat. Instead of a fearful path filled with road hazards, I saw a vast and inviting world of beauty and wonder.

I understood that God approved of my journey, but he did not intend for me to travel with an attitude of recklessness. I was free to explore and enjoy this God-world with a spirit of adventure, as long as I seasoned my choices with wisdom. What freedom to recognize all of creation as my playground, a place of discovery and pleasure!

I took the wheel and nestled comfortably back into the driver's seat. With scarcely a look backward, I confidently merged with the flow of traffic and began the journey of a lifetime.

A Word of Encouragement

Be strong and courageous.
Do not be afraid; do not be discouraged,
for the Lord your God
will be with you wherever you go.
Joshua 1:9

Dear Friend,

After four years and innumerable revisions, my story of the tunnel was complete, or so I thought.

Somehow I was not convinced that the story I was compelled to tell was finished. I could not share what I did not know, and that was how to live outside the tunnel. My story sat untouched for two more years.

I had to convey what my continued journey was teaching me. Healing is not the promise of fulfilled dreams, nor is it a guarantee of unwavering faith or the absence of heartache.

Along the way signs of brokenness will resurface—a fear here, a lingering memory there. At times it will seem that memories of those life-altering experiences will never be wiped away. On the other hand, how sad it would be if they were erased, only to carry with them all of the warm and treasured memories gathered along the way.

The dictionary definition of wholeness is to be sound in all aspects of human nature, specifically in physical, intellectual, and spiritual development. I learned that moving from brokenness to wholeness is a journey, not a step. The tunnel, for me, was an important part of that journey.

I learned that minor setbacks, doubt, and discouragement are not synonymous with failure. They are steps to maturity. I learned to get back up, dust myself off, and move forward with purpose. I came to understood that life is about tomorrow, not yesterday.

I trust that you too will benefit from this lesson that has helped me establish the course of my life beyond the tunnel. I encourage you to walk forward into your new life with confidence and expectation. The heartache you have experienced, in the hand of the master, is a tool to refine you and make you more fit for the journey ahead.

Know that your life is worth living, and view today as one step toward a better future. Above all, enjoy the journey!

Believing in your strength,
Your traveling partner

Afterword

Sadly, the starting point of my story is a common one. Time has not been successful in eliminating domestic violence from our culture. On occasion, with the advancement of video, an instance of physical abuse is captured for all to see. On these occasions, we are confronted with its reality and shocked by its severity. In error, we tend to assume that what we are seeing is an anomaly, both in terms of frequency and the level of cruelty.

Unfortunately, when the abuse is unseen, people seem to be cynical about its reality and prevalence. Perhaps it is too preposterous to believe, too ugly to accept. Perhaps women are still considered accountable for their victimization, either by their behavior or by their failure to remove themselves from a violent environment.

Regardless of perceptions, the facts speak for themselves. In 2015, the National Coalition Against Domestic Violence released another round of disturbing statistics: a woman is beaten every nine seconds in the United States; on a typical day, there are more than twenty-thousand phone calls placed to domestic violence hotlines nationwide; 19% of domestic violence cases involve a weapon; and only 34% of those injured by intimate partners seek medical care for their injuries. Even more shocking, three women are murdered every day as a result of domestic violence. In little more than a decade, that number equates to eighteen thousand women.

These statistics do not account for emotional abuse, that insidious and invisible method of breaking down the heart and mind of the abused, without leaving a visible trace.

I must admit, now so many years removed from a life of domestic violence, that I can no longer feel the hopelessness of those trapped in abusive relationships. I cannot feel their pain or relate to the terror they experience on a daily basis. I can testify, however, that domestic violence is real and that it can be life-threatening. At its best, for those who do escape, it is a traumatic experience that paves the way for a lifetime battle for self-worth.

There is no easy answer, but there are steps we can take. We can be aware that domestic violence is occurring under our noses, so to speak. We can watch for the unspoken pleas for help. We can respond carefully to words that might be verbalized only once. We can believe stories that seem preposterous. We can put away doubt and judgment, and we can respond with compassion and patience.

We can be *Liv* to someone in need.

---

[1] National Coalition Against Domestic Violence (NCADV), *2016 National Statistics*. http://www.ncadv.org/learn/statistics.

Acknowledgments

I woke early one morning with the distinct impression that I must capture on paper the emotional roller coaster of divorce. That impression quickly became a driving force. For days on end, I used the keyboard to expel each of my deepest feelings into written form. I shared my idea and my initial chapters with friends. As good friends do, they encouraged me to continue writing.

Initially I viewed the writing process as an agent of personal healing. Only after I believed that I would escape the darkness and begin to love life did I want to share this hope with others.

One difference in my second journey through grief was my support system, a resource I had never before effectively tapped. My friends and family encompassed me; they upheld me emotionally, financially, and spiritually. In putting my experiences on paper, I honor their devotion and selflessness. Many people helped me along the way, and at the risk of overlooking some I mention a few.

Some friends are many miles but only a heartbeat away. I can only hope to be the kind of friend they have been to me. Collectively they are Liv, the friend addressed at the end of each chapter. Amy walked with me through the toughest of times. Our friendship was forged in the fire, and because of that it is pure and lasting. Elizabeth has always been my greatest fan. She showers me with love and loyalty, and I know God smiles on her for the way she befriends his children. Barb is my forever-steady friend. Her quiet, reliable, and compassionate friendship has always brought balance to my out-of-kilter life.

The family that I rejoined helped to pick up the pieces of my life and never said, "I told you so." My brother and his wife made their home our home. My mom and dad, though their hearts were broken, stayed strong to help me along. My sister checked on me each day to make sure all my needs were met. My niece served as chauffeur, helping me start my new life in the right direction, literally.

Others along the way gave me opportunity to use my voice, and their support helped me regain my confidence. Some laughed with me through the many challenges that seemed to plague my life, and new friends encouraged me to write and patiently nurtured my faith.

My children played a unique role in my journey. Only when I was far outside the tunnel did I begin to understand the magnitude of turmoil that had been stirred in their lives because of my decisions and circumstances. That realization became a greater heartache than my own troubles. Through it all, however, each made contributions to my healing that still warm my heart. Caleb gave his loyalty and advice, encouraging me to move on with my life when I could not even imagine the road ahead. Michael kept a protective watch over me and his sisters. He played his part in our "family meetings," made sure we had all the comfort he could provide, and always found ways to make us smile. Kaitlyn held onto a beauty and enthusiasm that no circumstance could dim, and I learned to admire her for it. Stephanie helped keep the household in order, and she used her quick wit to keep me challenged and laughing.

Carla became my newest friend and traveling companion. Together we came to understand that life is an adventure, and it doesn't matter so much if we get lost along the way.

Near the end of my six-year writing journey, I was blessed with a healthy relationship and a lifetime commitment for which I am so grateful. My husband, Bob, has quietly supported me, patiently encouraged me to dig through the past, and understood that this is a story I must tell.

Here's to family, friendship, and a restored life!

About the Author

There is no question that *Twice Broken* is an abridged retelling of author Kathleen Serenko's life. It was never intended, however, to be a memoir. What began as an exercise of healing became a passion to connect with others living in the midst of grief.

Kathleen spent much of her career in education, corporate training and communications. As a business owner, she now helps companies develop and execute communications and public relations strategies. She also writes industry content for a number of manufacturing, financial and trade publications. She is a trained public speaker and facilitator.

Kathleen is the mother of four adult children, and she resides in Pennsylvania with her husband. She is currently working on her second book, *Another Crazy Day.*

Additional details are available at www.TwiceBroken.org.

CPSIA information can be obtained
at www.ICGtesting.com
Printed in the USA
LVOW08s2217220617
539095LV00002B/156/P